CW00409001

Portrait of -
WARRINGTON

Jen Darling

SIGMA LEISURE
Wilmslow, United Kingdom

First published in 1989 by
Reprinted 1990
Sigma Leisure, an imprint of **Sigma Press** 1 South Oak Lane, Wilmslow, SK9 6AR, England.

British Library Cataloguing in Publication Data
A CIP catalogue record for this book is available from the British Library.

ISBN: 1-85058-207-6

Typesetting and design by
Sigma Hi-Tech Services Ltd

Printed by:
Manchester Free Press

Front Cover:
Warrington Market Place in 1834 - taken from Baine's "Lancashire", with permission from Warrington Library

Preface

This book is one of Sigma Leisure's 'Portrait' series of towns in the North West, and it is hoped that a portrait of Warrington's diverse development will be built up throughout its pages. Similarly, an artist might build up his knowledge of a person by first looking at a picture from babyhood, another of the developing child, and then the mature adult - warts and all!

All Warringtonians owe a debt of gratitude to many people, not least the Warrington Society and the Friends of Warrington who, in the past, were responsible for the many plaques on buildings of historical significance around the town. We are also indebted to the supporters of churches, and to citizens that have fought, often against the odds, to preserve our heritage.

I would like to thank the staff at the Library and Museum, particularly David Rogers, who took the time to offer literature and help at the beginning to a very raw recruit, and Sylvia Wright and Peter Rogerson who have patiently answered my many requests for information. I am also indebted to many local people who gave me information about the town, and an especial thank you to Paddy O'Brien for reading the text, and making many pertinent comments.

On the pictorial side I would like to thank the *Warrington Guardian* for printing my original plea for help, The Warrington Photographic Society, Alison Yarwood from the Warrington New Town Development Corporation, the Editor of *Cheshire Life*, the Deputy Regional Director of the National Westminster Bank, and the following local people who offered material so readily:

Mr G. Atkinson, Mr T. Birchall, Mr G. Bradley, Mrs Davies, Mrs D. Devlin, Mr R. Dowd, Mr R. Glover, Mr J. Hamlett, Mr P. Moss, Mr M. Nicholas, Mr J.W. Norbury, Mrs Patton, Mrs E. Sankey, Mr and Mrs R. Smith, Mr G. Tickle, Mr A. Weston, Mr B. Yates.

And finally, an especial word of thanks to my two main photographers - Mr A.E. Howell and Jack Gregory.

ANNO
DECIMO
VICTORIÆ
REGINÆ

DEUS DAT INCREMENTUM

The Town Hall and
gates - reproduced with
permission from John
Cocks for *Cheshire Life*.

CONTENTS

Introduction

Success Through Diversity

Perhaps the word 'diverse' best describes the town of Warrington - one of the oldest in the North West.

Even the explanations of the word Warrington are diverse. Did it originate from the Roman settlement at Wilderspool known as Veratinum? Is it derived from the Saxon word *'woering'* meaning a rampart, and the ancient English *'tun'* - a town? In old English the word *'waer'* meant a dam or weir, and *'werid'* meant a ford. Therefore, does Warrington mean the town at the ford, or the weir? *'Waer'* may even have been the name of a tribe living in these parts, so was Warrington once Waer's town? And, to add further to the confusion, in the Domesday Book of 1086 Warrington is referred to as *Walintune*.

Despite this confusion over the origin of its name, there is certainly no doubt as to the diversity of the transport system leading from it, stemming from ancient times when its position was recorded thus:

'At the head of the estuary, just above the tidal limit, in one of the last of its loops, was a wide and shallow section where it could be crossed on foot. Primitive man established a ford here (near Black Bear Bridge). Small settlements sprang up on higher ground to north and south.'

This quote gives the main reason for a settlement in the Warrington area; the first organised settlement in Roman times growing up south of the river, while the later town developed on the north bank, so that nowadays Warrington occupies a strategic position astride the Mersey.

Its situation has led to its development as the natural gateway to other parts of the country, and to its title as 'The Hub of the North West'. Certainly, routes radiate from it through Chester and on to North Wales, through Cheshire and on to the Midlands and the South, through Lancashire and on to Cumbria and Scotland, while, locally, equidistant 'spokes' reach Liverpool to the west and Manchester to the east, and soon fast motorway routes will link it to the Channel tunnel and out into Europe.

A further outstanding feature in the development of Warrington is the diversity of its industry. Since Roman times it has been a town of many industries; even during the Industrial Revolution, when other north-west towns concentrated solely on one industry (often cotton), Warrington had its brewers, its wire workers, its soap manufacturers, its tool makers and its tanners.

More recently, Warrington's development as a New Town has been heralded as its second

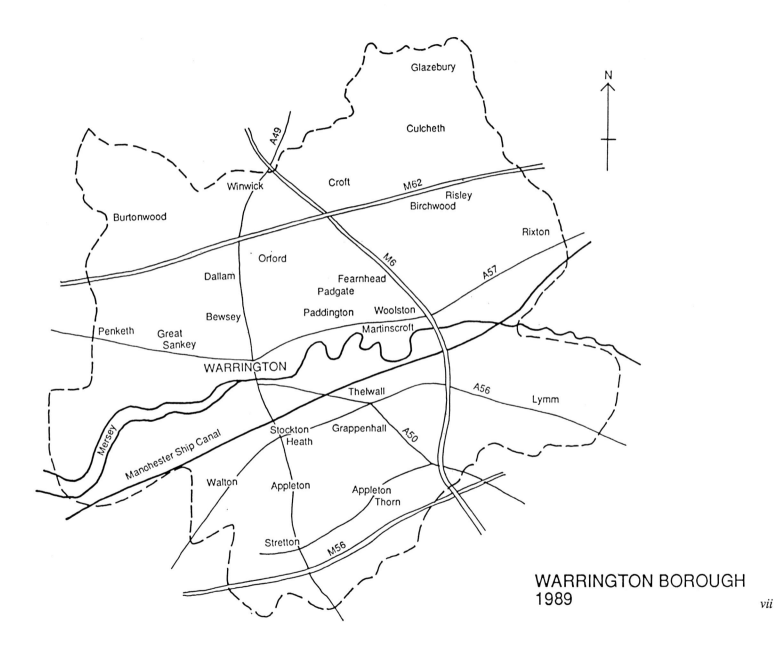

WARRINGTON BOROUGH
1989

Industrial Revolution, and certainly, since it was first brought to the public's attention, diverse has been local opinion about it! After its inception in 1969, the *Warrington Guardian* reported,

'The New Town is welcomed by those who admit its foresightedness and boldness of design, but opposed by those whose properties will be demolished or reduced in value, and who are unimpressed by the experience of similar 'New Towns' in other parts of the country.'

Diverse have certainly been the New Town's activities. A huge amount of new industry has been attracted to the area, both from the home market and abroad. Derelict land has been reclaimed in several areas to the north of the Mersey, supporting a variety of new housing with excellent amenities. Also, attractive linear parks have quelled, to some extent, the fears of country lovers that the New Town would destroy the little natural beauty of the region. Hopefully, the good work is not going to be tainted by a huge suburban sprawl of executive homes to the south as the New Town seeks to recoup money for the Government in a final burst of activity.

In trying to build up a picture of the town from the wealth of material available, a wide range of diverse subject matter has been covered. Interesting facets of history have been extracted where something remains to link the present with the past, whether it be simply a street name, a plaque, or a building sympathetically restored. Similarly, with the industry and leisure sections, yesterday has, wherever possible, been linked with today. So, it is hoped that as the pages are turned, a clear and interesting picture of the town will emerge.

Chapter 1: History

Ancient Times

Ten thousand years ago ice covered all of northern England, and it seems appropriate to start the story of Warrington with a relic left behind from this far-distant time. It is a sizable, mottled boulder - an erratic - standing outside Scholl's Footwear Shop just off Buttermarket Street. As the Ice Age receded large stones like this one were sometimes dragged along the pebbled ground, one surface worn smooth by the friction thus generated.

As the climate warmed early man came to Britain and, displayed in our Museum, are finds that show us that he lived around the Warrington area. Flints dating back to the Stone Age come from Orford and Stockton Heath and, when the Manchester Ship Canal was excavated, dug-out canoes from this time were also discovered. Relics from the Bronze Age, unearthed in several areas of the town, include a macabre find at Grappenhall early this century of a number of burial urns, inside which were charred human bones.

The earliest organised settlement in the area was the Roman fortified town of Veratinum

An erratic - relic from the Ice Age.
A.E. Howell

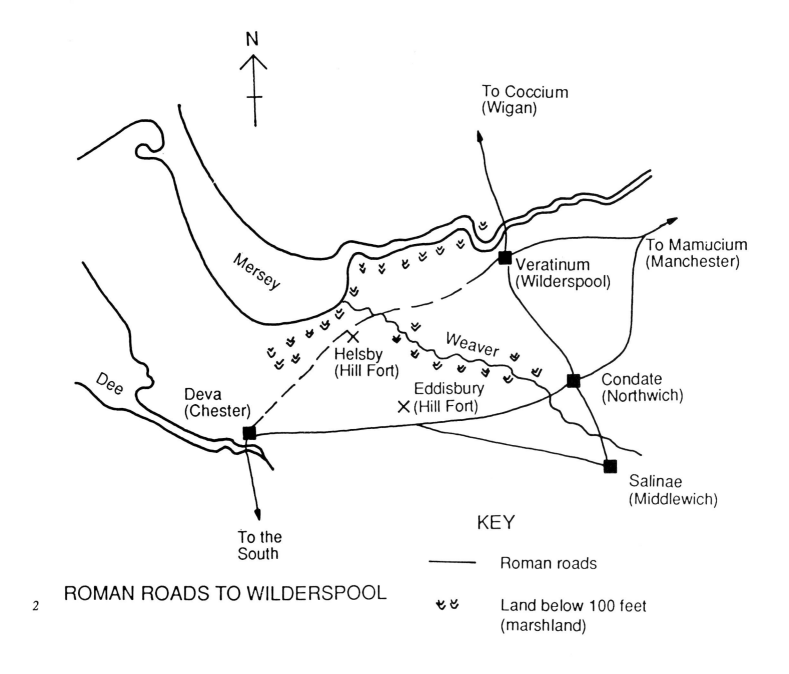

N

To Coccium
(Wigan)

Mersey

To Mamucium
(Manchester)

Veratinum
(Wilderspool)

Weaver

Helsby
(Hill Fort)

Dee

Eddisbury
X (Hill Fort)

Condate
(Northwich)

Deva
(Chester)

Salinae
(Middlewich)

To the
South

KEY

———— Roman roads

ROMAN ROADS TO WILDERSPOOL

2

Land below 100 feet
(marshland)

which grew up on the south bank of the River Mersey at Wilderspool and Stockton Heath, near the first fordable point of the river. The Roman road here is thought to have followed the line of Loushers Lane to Latchford, where the ford, thought to be situated at the far end of Wash Lane, could be crossed twice daily at low tides. The loop of the Mersey used to be much more pronounced here, and the road went west to School Brow before turning north along Winwick Road (now the A49) and on to the fort at Wigan (Coccium).

The road south from Veratinum passed through Stockton Heath, Hill Cliffe and Stretton, en route to Northwich (Condate). Another road went east to Manchester (Mamucium) and, almost certainly, one ran west to the large fortified settlement of Chester (Deva). Thus Warrington was, even in those far distant times, a road junction linked to all the major Roman settlements in the North West.

It was in Loushers Lane that the remains of a Roman house were discovered this century with part of a Roman underfloor central heating system - a hypocaust. And this is thought to have been the 'upper-class', residential area of the time.

The oval plaque on the Greenall Whitley brewery is easily spotted as you cross the swing bridge from Stockton Heath. It states that the brewery stands on the site of the Roman station which was occupied from about AD75 to AD410. Many industrial finds discovered here date from Roman times, including an unusual bronze ruler. Another unique discovery was an

EDWARD THE ELDER FOUNDED A CYTY
HERE AND CALLED IT THELWALL

almost entire actor's mask which can be seen in the Museum. The mask, made from local clay, represents Tragedy, and is the only example of its kind to be found in Britain.

A Roman legion made its base nestling under Hill Cliffe at Stockton Heath where, near Roman Road, the remains of a temple with an altar, and bust of Minerva, Roman goddess of Wisdom and patron of Arts and Crafts, were discovered this century.

With the departure of the Romans from the region in the 4th century, there was much conflict in the area, these years being known as the Dark Ages when the Picts and Scots vied with the Saxons, and the Northumbrians fought the Mercians.

It was in the 7th century that the Christian king Oswald, who ruled Northumbria, fought the pagan king Penda from Mercia (Wales). In one of their battles Oswald was slain, and a relic from this time is a Saxon cross in Winwick church which shows his dismemberment. Also, St. Oswald's well in Hermitage Green is claimed by some to have been the death place of this famous king and saint. The depression left behind after the battle is supposed to have formed a well filled with water said to have special healing powers.

Late in the Saxon period, Edward the Elder ruled much of the country, establishing a settlement at Thelwall when his troops were aiming to repel the Danes and make the area safe for the Saxons. Records show that the King visited Thelwall in the late summer of AD923, and the writing on the Pickering Arms also testifies this. On that visit he ordered the city to be rebuilt and protected from Danish raids.

A century later, Paganus de Vilars became the first Lord of the Manor, and the Domesday Survey of 1086 mentions Warrington and its surroundings as being worth £4 10s!

By the 13th century a settlement north of the Mersey was established - on Mote Hill (near the parish church). This area has since been levelled but at that time it had two important advantages as a site for a new settlement. It was the only point in the area above flood level, and it was on the old Roman road. An agricultural community grew up here with a population of about 120, the only buildings probably being a wooden church, a moated manor house, and a few small timber cottages.

Paganus de Vilars also ruled over the manors of Little Sankey, Orford and Howley, and his grand-daughter married a de Boteler who was butler to the Earl of Chester - hence the origin of the name, Boteler. It was in AD1260, when their home on Mote Hill was burnt down, that the family decided to move to Bewsey. The word itself actually means 'beautiful site' and Bewsey Manor was built there in 1264.

The Boteler family continued to rule over the town for 18 generations, and one Sir Thomas le Boteler established the first Boteler Grammar School in Bag Lane (now School Brow).

Christians Awake!

The Friary. In the middle of the 13th century Friars of the Order of St. Augustine were granted land at Bridgefoot on which to build a friary. This was known as the Jesus Church, and stood in the area between St Austin's Lane and Bridge Street where a plaque still marks its site. During the Civil War Royalists burnt it down and it was later replaced by the Anglicans with Holy Trinity. However, the street names of Friars Gate and St. Austin's Lane are constant reminders of the religious house that once stood here, and the recently built Postern Gate pub, has taken its name from the back entrance to The Friary where the poor would come for food and drink.

The Augustinian Hermit Friars were an order devoted to teaching, the cure of souls, and missions. They wore black and white habits at that time, with long, wide sleeves, a black leather girdle, and a long pointed cowl reaching to the waist. One of their number, an erudite scholar called Friar Penketh, is even mentioned in Shakespeare's Richard III.

The Anglicans. St. Elphin's, Warrington's first parish church, was built on Mote Hill late in AD675. It is thought that a Welsh monk from the monastic college of Bangor-on-Dee came as a missionary to Warrington where he converted the local people to Christianity. Certainly, St. Elphin's is mentioned in the Domesday Survey of 1086, and is the only church in Britain named after this saint, who has never been officially canonised. The building of that time would have been a simple structure of rough-hewn wood, and was probably on the site of the present church.

The church now standing dates from 1226, the oldest stonework, composed of rough hewn blocks of Norman origin, being at the east end. Much of the church was rebuilt late in the 14th century by Sir William le Boteler (9th Baron). There are many memorials to the Patten family, including a recumbent marble figure of John Wilson Patten who sold the Town Hall to the Borough.

The spire was only added in 1860 and is the third tallest church spire in England. It is crowned with a weathercock gilded with golden sovereigns, and the Rector at that time devised a slogan 'a guinea for a golden cock' to raise funds to pay for it.

In 1943 the former Boteler Chapel was transformed by intricately carved oak panelling, and the installation of many ceremonial flags and regalia, into the South Lancashire Regimental Chapel because of this Regiment's long and special association with Warrington.

The eight bells were recast, and a new clock given, as a memorial to Sir Peter Rylands who died on the eve of his 80th birthday in 1948. Today, the mellow notes strike the hour, and the eight computerised bells are even programmed to play a hymn tune.

Holy Trinity, the church at Market Gate, was built in 1709 and, like the Town Hall, was

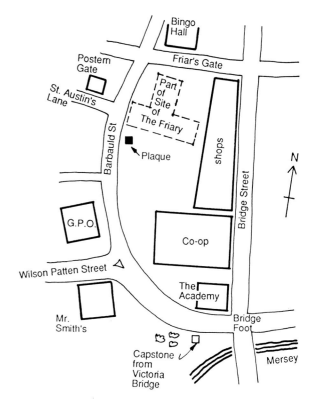

LOCATION OF THE FRIARY

5

St. Wilfrid's, Grappenhall, dominates the cobbled village
street.
A.E. Howell

St. Oswald's, Winwick - on the tower wall a pig stands
beside St. Anthony.
A.E. Howell

Prominent landmark - the clock which belongs to the
Borough and tops Holy Trinity church tower.
A.E. Howell

The soaring spire of Warrington's Parish Church.
A.E. Howell

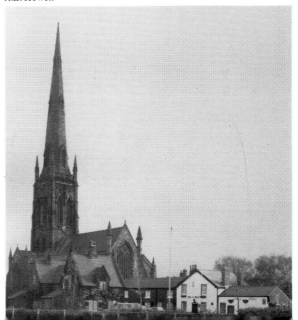

designed by James Gibbs. Its stone tower, which stands astride a public passageway, belongs to the church, while the wooden structure on top housing the town clock belongs to the Borough. The clock strikes the hour on a bell that was given to the town as a curfew bell in 1647. This was first placed in the Court House in the market place, and was then used as a fire bell for a time before ending up in its lofty perch here. Resplendent above the central aisle of the church is a brass candelabra which once hung in the House of Commons.

This sturdy building, its walls of sandstone blocks, is very much a town centre church. In addition to Sunday services it holds a Communion Service on Thursday morning, a service for shoppers each Friday afternoon, and coffee is served every morning to those who seek a few minutes respite from the bustle of the busy town.

Another church still remembered is **St. Paul's** which was built in 1830 from Hill Cliffe red sandstone of very poor quality, and, when dry rot was discovered in the fabric, it was demolished.

The original **St. James'** church stood in Knutsford Road, only moving to its present site in 1829. The site was donated by Thomas Lyon, and the large Victorian vicarage still stands opposite, now occupied by Laycocks'. Huge and badly designed, it was originally built by the owner of Artingstall's Brush Works as his family home, and became known as Artingstall's folly. It was also reputed to be haunted.

The village of **Winwick** has grown up on the site of an ancient Saxon settlement, and the cross-arm of a Celtic preaching cross, which is over 1000 years old, is now preserved in the church. This cross would have stood on top of the hill long before there was any religious building there. However, a church at Winwick, dedicated to St. Oswald, is mentioned in the Domesday Book in 1086. At that time the living was owned by Roger of Poitou, one of William the Conqueror's nobles. It later passed under the patronage of Nostel Priory before being owned by the Derby family, by which time it was a very wealthy living.

Parts of the present building, which is made of local sandstone, date from 1330, and a 14th century font, perhaps damaged in the Civil War, can still be seen. Near it is a copy of the Vinegar Bible - so named because of a misprint in the heading to the twentieth chapter of St. Luke's Gospel where the word 'vinegar' has been printed instead of 'vineyard', thus making the title 'The Parable of the Vinegar'! Nearby too, in the richly-coloured east window of the north aisle, the story of King Oswald's life is depicted in stained glass.

There are several intriguing explanations concerning the carving of the pig with the bell round its neck to be found on the west wall of the tower. One is that a pig was used to move the stones to this place when the chosen site for the church was altered. A second is that it was the stonemason's cryptic way of putting the initials of St. Oswald's Winwick (SOW) on the church.

Perhaps the most plausible is that the niche to the left of the pig contains the image of St. Antony, whose mascot was a pig.

Welby Pugin, who had a share in the building of the Houses of Parliament, designed the chancel which was rebuilt in the mid-1800s, and, in the Peter Legh chapel, there are brasses of Peter Legh and his wife. After her untimely death he became a priest, and is depicted wearing a priest's vestments together with full armour, sword and spurs - a rare combination.

It is thought that the first church was built in **Grappenhall** in 1120, and records confirm that a Norman church was already established there in 1189, with some of the stonework still incorporated into the structure of the present building. The rare, rectangular, sandstone font is also thought to be Norman, and there is a Norman chest rough hewn from the trunk of an oak tree. The medieval stained glass window has been called the 'jewel in the crown' of the present church, and visitors from far afield come to admire its splendour.

Some think that the black cat carved in stone on the west wall of the tower is the original Cheshire cat. Certainly Lewis Carroll, son of a Daresbury vicar, often visited Grappenhall as a child, and this carving may have given him the idea for the character in his 'Alice' books. The stocks by the gate are also a reminder of bygone times.

All Saints Church, Thelwall, was built in 1843 and all its windows are of stained glass. One particular window was dedicated in 1950 to the memory of Sir Peter Rylands and his wife, and it shows the Rylands crest and a wiredrawer at his bench.

Nonconformity. The Presbyterians built the first Nonconformist church in Warrington in Sankey Street at the beginning of the 18th century. It was replaced by the present building, now known as Cairo Street Chapel, in 1745. Several of its early ministers were also tutors at the Academy, and both tutors and students regularly worshipped there. Inside is a memorial plaque to John Aikin, Rector of the Academy, and an antique chair used by him. There is also a most unusual, triangular chair which once belonged to Joseph Priestley, and a Wedgwood medallion depicting him can be viewed on enquiry.

Memorials can also be found to the Gaskell family of Latchford. A son, William, married Elizabeth (the novelist - Mrs Gaskell) and their infant son, who died of scarlet fever aged 9 months, is buried in the graveyard. Another memorial is to Frederick Monks, the local industrialist, who presented the Town Hall gates and the Oliver Cromwell statue to the Borough, and who worshipped there.

The Baptists of Hill Cliffe were an early group of Dissenters in the Warrington area, land for their burial ground being given to them in 1663 by a gentleman called John Morris, who came from Grappenhall. The oldest gravestone is that of Maria Heslop who died in 1664, and any that bear earlier dates are thought to be forgeries.

The pulpit Bible, printed in 1638, is five years older than the chapel which was not licensed for church services until 50 years later. The first minister was the Rev. Warburton of Arley, who was both pastor and soldier, and his walking stick is still in existence. It was not until the middle of the 19th century that the minister's house was built adjoining the church, and the burial ground was enclosed by the substantial stone wall which borders Red Lane today.

Perhaps the most popular local belief associated with the chapel is that Oliver Cromwell worshipped there during the Civil War. Some say he even read the lesson for morning service.

The Congs! Built at the end of the 18th century, Stepney Chapel in Flag Lane was the first Congregational church established in Warrington. It was followed by the original Wycliffe Church, which soon proved too small and was replaced by the present building in 1873. Built in Italian, Gothic style, the high square tower with its pyramid roof used to be seen from many parts of Warrington. Inside, notable features are the carved oak pulpit and the communion table made of wood from the Holy Land.

The Quakers. George Fox, the founder of the Quakers, also founded the Friends Meeting House at Penketh, which is surrounded by many gravestones of the Crosfield family, and is

Taken in 1906, Miss Clayton frowns over her 52 charges outside the school attached to the Working Men's Mission in Thewlis Street.

now used as a community centre. In the 19th century there was also a large Quaker school (now an old people's home) in Stocks Lane.

Early in the 18th century came the first building of the Friends Meeting House at Buttermarket Street, and this was replaced in 1830 by the present building which was completed for £800. Wrought iron gates lead into a Garden of Rest, where memorial tablets to several members of the Crosfield family are to be found, together with the grave of Joseph Crosfield, founder of the soapworks at Bank Quay.

Workingsmen's Mission. John Crosfield, youngest son of Joseph, established a Town Mission in 1862, having heard how a small group of his soap workers met for weekly prayer in the kitchen of a cottage in Factory Yard. Although closed in 1869, this was the fore-runner of the Workingmen's Mission, soon established on Liverpool Road at a cost of just over £500.

John Crosfield continued to finance this enterprise and, in 1898, a new infants school was also built on Thewlis Street. When the old chapel was demolished in 1901 after his death, his wife contributed half the cost of the new church, and this simple, red brick chapel, surrounded by its pretty garden, was opened for public worship by her in February 1904.

Methodism. In the middle of the 18th century John Wesley preached in Warrington on at least two occasions, and the enthusiasm he engendered led to the founding of Methodism in the town. Before 1779 when the first Wesleyan Methodist Church was built in Upper Bank Street, worshippers met in the Old Malt Kiln in Back Dallam Lane.

In the middle of the 19th century a new, much larger church was built in Bold Street. With walls composed of huge chunks of Hill Cliffe sandstone several feet thick, this church was definitely made to last. It seated 1300 people - the large box pews rented by families encircled by a spacious gallery. There were also two ministers' houses, several small rooms, and a hall, where both Yehudi Menuhin and Isobel Bailey gave recitals, but which usually accommodated over 500 Sunday School scholars.

This building was demolished with great difficulty in 1973 and was replaced by the modern building we see today. At this time some of the land was released and an office block replaced the ministers' houses. It is an interesting reflection on rising prices that the 1849 church cost £4,000 to build, while the 1973 church, together with the office complex, totalled £400,000.

The new church, which seats 250, has both a minister's and a caretaker's flat attached, plus a large hall and other rooms that house the Sunday School and Youth Club. Good work is done in the community with lunch clubs for the elderly, Saturday coffee mornings for shoppers, and many other activities taking place.

The **Independent Methodists**, worshipping in Providence Chapel, Stockton Heath, set up the first total Abstinence Society in England in 1830. Soon after this Friar's Green chapel was built - the very first home of Independent Methodism. In its early days, publicans' agents would disrupt the sermon by handing round buckets of free beer to the congregation.

Catholicism. Like the Methodists, the Catholics used the Old Malt Kiln in Back Dallam Lane for worship for a time. Later **St. Alban's** Church was built in Bewsey Street in 1823, and is the oldest Roman Catholic church in Warrington today. The altar is very striking, made of a solid slab of polished marble supported by marble pillars.

In 1877 the light and airy church of **St. Mary**, with its pale sandstone exterior, was built on the site of an old cotton mill that had been burnt down. Later, the old dispensary was bought to add to the church buildings and was, for a time, a convent. In August 1977 Cardinal Basil Hume, then the Roman Catholic Archbishop of Westminster, came to celebrate the centenary.

The Salvation Army began its work in Warrington in April 1883, although its magazine *'War Cry'* had been sold in the town before this. Its arrival had a mixed response, with the Mayor at that time - John Crosfield - ordering the covering up of its advertisements, which simply led to more publicity. Controversy raged in the Press for and against the Army for a long time, but it was also noticeable that drunken brawls began to diminish.

Its first citadel was in an old malt kiln in Academy Street which could only hold 500 people crammed on wood and iron benches. The interior was forbidding with dark panelled walls, and flaring gas jets provided the only illumination. The building was so decrepit that even the floor had to be strengthened before it could support a congregation. A procession through the streets preceded each meeting, and this used to attract such a crowd that many were often left outside.

The members soon formed their own brass band which had a very mixed reception, the public covering their ears or, worse still, flinging fish or mud at the bandsmen. As the band's repertoire was limited to one tune, and the instruments often needed repairing, particularly the drum, perhaps this reaction was, to some extent, understandable! The band's first uniform was composed of cast-off artillery tunics decorated by somewhat tatty yellow facings. One bandsman decided to brighten these up with yellow chalk which, unfortunately, washed off in the rain!

Since its arrival in the town, the Army has always taken part in Walking Day, and 'outposts' in Orford Lane, Latchford and Stockton Heath were established throughout their first summer. This zeal was soon rewarded by a visit from William Booth, the Army's founder.

Although the Malt Kiln was enlarged in 1932, with an imposing facade fronting onto Buttermarket Street, the structure soon deteriorated and the building was demolished in 1981. Bell Hall in Orford Lane was used for three years before the imposing, purpose-built premises were opened in Academy Street in May 1982. This building, designed by Mr Pat Garrett, acts as a Citadel and a Community Centre, with Day Care services, a luncheon club for pensioners, a Mums' and Toddlers' group, and various other organisations all using the facilities.

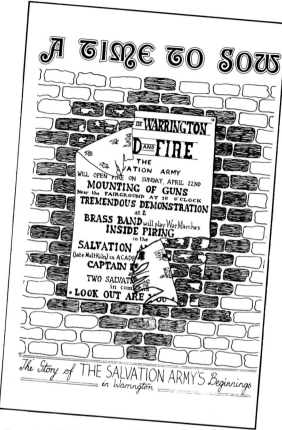

Posters heralded the controversial arrival of the Salvation Army in Warrington.

11

Resplendent at Bridge Foot stands the bronze statue of Oliver Cromwell, donated to the town by Frederick Monks.
A.E. Howell

In these ecumenical days of high costs several denominations sometimes agree to share church buildings. This has occurred in Westbrook where the Anglicans and Methodists share a church, and at Locking Stumps where the **Thomas Risley Church** has a joint congregation of Baptists, Methodists and United Reformists.

The original Thomas Risley church was founded in 1662, but the building, demolished to make way for the M62 in 1979, dated from 1707. In compensation the Department of the Environment agreed to build a new 'free' church and the bell, pulpit and stone font has been incorporated into this. It is a true community church having, among other activities, a play-school meeting five mornings a week.

Off to War

Warrington has good reason to be proud of the way its citizens have fought for their country, men from the town having been involved in fighting as far back as the Crusades and the Wars of the Roses.

However, Warrington has also profited from War. Arrows made in the town were used against the Scots at the Battle of Flodden, and the firms of Rylands and Gaskells made at least half the canvass for the Royal Navy during the French Wars and the Napoleonic Wars. Rylands also made a vast fortune manufacturing barbed wire for the Western Front during the First World War, and added to this during the Second World War by manufacturing aircraft wings, anti-submarine nets and nets for torpedoes and mine sweepers.

Warrington was the scene of several skirmishes in the **Civil War** years. Near the beginning, when the Royalists led by Lord Derby had the upper hand, there was fighting at Stockton Heath.

The oldest pub in the town - the Black Horse at Sankey Bridges, which dates from 1632 - was also involved in the Civil War. The house was used by the Earl of Derby as the headquarters of the Royalist army. It was fiercely attacked by Parliamentary troops in 1643 until the Earl threatened to burn down the entire town centre and the bridge over the Mersey.

At the end of the Civil War many Royalists had to pay heavy fines to get back their property. Edward Bridgeman, the owner of the Black Horse, was no exception, having to pay £100 for its return. The impressive herringbone design in its gables was common to wealthy families, and it still has the original low ceilings and thick timber beams - some of which are rumoured to have come from Nelson's flagship, the Victory. Later, the Black Horse became a coaching inn on the main road from Warrington to Liverpool.

There was also a battle at Winwick in 1648, when Cromwell and his Parliamentarians chased a Scottish army of Royalists from Preston down to Warrington Bridge, where they

Taken in 1898, the Black Horse at Sankey Bridges is the oldest pub in Warrington.
F.W. Knowles

Oliver Cromwell lodged on the site of the General Wolfe Inn pictured here.
A E. Howell

finally surrendered. During this confrontation there was much fighting in the Parish Church area, and circular indentations, still visible in the outside wall of the chancel, were made by cannon balls fired by the Roundheads.

Victorious, Cromwell addressed both his troops and his Scottish prisoners on Pyghill (an area near where the Waysiders now stands), before sending the latter home along a lane which is still called Scotland Road. Afterwards, Cromwell lodged for the night in Church Street in a building that stood on the site of the General Wolfe Inn.

In 1651 King Charles II, accompanied by the Duke of Buckingham, fought in a skirmish on Warrington Bridge, and later that year the Earl of Derby, abject in defeat, crossed the Bridge on his way to execution at Bolton.

The statue of Oliver Cromwell, now standing beside the Academy at Bridge Foot, was presented to the town by Frederick Monks in 1899 to commemorate the ter-centenary of Cromwell's birth. There he looks likely to remain, although controversy still rages as to whether this famous leader should be honoured or abhorred. He was certainly a hard man, prisoners often being treated with great cruelty or sold into slavery.

A memorial to all those men who died in the Boer War at the turn of the century is to be found in Queen's Gardens. The bronze statue is of **Lieutenant-Colonel O'Leary** who, mortally wounded while leading the victorious charge at Pieter's Hill, shouted the immortal words, 'Remember, men, the eyes of Lancashire are watching you.'

As so often happens, the town was slow to erect a memorial and, typically, the plea for funds

13

from Alderman Arthur Bennett (Mayor, chartered accountant, resident of Paddington House and poet) was in verse form:

> Refrain from the 'Song of the Forgotten Dead'.
> *You have money for your football, your tobacco and your beer,*
> *And you know the lives of hardship that we led;*
> *But we saved an Empire for you, and are lying voiceless here -*
> *Have you nothing to commemorate your dead!*

Completed in 1875, the **Peninsula Barracks** acts as a reminder that Warrington was once a garrison town. When first built, it stood at the edge of the town surrounded by fields which, in 1971, led an ex-Warringtonian to write,

'I can still hear the sound of the bugle and the tramp of hob-nailed boots. I can also hear the sound of the mowing machine in the field opposite the barrack gate ...'

Until the 1960s the Peninsula Barracks was home to the **South Lancashire Regiment** which took an active part in the Seven Years' War, the American War of Independence, the Napoleonic Wars and the Boer War, as well as the two World Wars.

In 1947 the Prime Minister, Clement Attlee, paid a special visit to Warrington when he unveiled the stained glass window in the Parish Church, erected as a memorial to the men from the South Lancashire Regiment who lost their lives in the Second World War. Since then battle honours from the Regiment have been deposited in the Church, and a plaque, dated September 1947, further emphasises the town's close links with the Regiment. It states that Warrington Borough Council request the Regiment to march through the streets of Warrington with 'drums beating, bands playing, colours flying and bayonets fixed' on all ceremonial occasions.

Nowadays, the massive hulk of the Barracks is used as a cadet training school and houses a small regimental museum.

Burtonwood Airforce Base. Although at one time the area of Burtonwood was an extensive forest, by this century most of the woodland had been cleared and, in 1938, a site for an airfield was selected here because it comprised flat farmland with good drainage, was close to towns and industry, and next to a railway line. With the outbreak of war this site was developed rapidly and became the largest military establishment outside the USA.

In 1942, technicians from Texas arrived causing quite a stir with their outlandish clothes and ways, and these were soon followed by American soldiers. Famous celebrities who visited Burtonwood during the war years to keep up the American's spirits included Bing Crosby, Bob Hope and James Cagney.

The O'Leary statue in Queen's Gardens -
`Remember men the eyes of Lancashire are watching you.'.
A.E. Howell

In 1946, the United States Air Force base at Burtonwood was handed back to the RAF, although the USA Air Force was back two years later to service aircraft for the Berlin Airlift. However, use of the Base has gradually dwindled, the M62 now runs along what was once the main runway, and the American Air Force are no longer 'in situ'. In 1989, the Duke of Westminster visited America in an attempt to attract new industry to this derelict area awaiting development.

Padgate RAF Camp was established as a transit camp during the Second World War, when many Britons made a first brief encounter with Warrington. Nowadays, Padgate High School and modern housing cover much of its site.

The men who were members of **Padgate Home Guard** are sure that the popular television series was based on them. One of their members can still remember playing halfpenny brag when they were on duty at night, and tells of the hot pot supper that took place at the outdoor swimming pool known as the Lido at Woolston.

Royal Ordnance Factory at Risley. Over 30,000 people worked day and night at this factory for the duration of the Second World War. There was a workers' hostel, and many women worked in the Munitions Factory where they could earn as much as £4 per week. In fact, there was a vast recruitment campaign aimed at women workers, as this advertisement shows:

15

WAR WORK - AN APPEAL TO WOMEN

Women are wanted for war work
To make the arms we need.
They're wanted from shop and household,
So that Britain may take the lead.
.....
You will make our guns and shells,
Our aircraft and our tanks.
Your work will bring us victory,
And earn the nation's thanks.

Anon

The factory was closed after the War when it took £2.5m to demolish the derelict buildings. Today grassy mounds in Birchwood Forest Park provide the only evidence of the four bunkers which once extended deep underground, and the reservoir which supplied water to the factory is a secluded walled garden.

Civilian casualties in the town during the last War were few, but one tragedy took place in September 1940 when, during a garden fete, a solitary German raider off-loaded his bombs on Thames Board Mills recreation ground killing fifteen civilians.

The Warrington people sacrificed their town in other ways too. When iron was needed for armaments the Arpley cannons, relics of the Crimean War went, together with a tank from Victoria Park used in the First World War. Bank Park railings were removed and, perhaps the biggest sacrifice of all in this respect, was the melting down of the magnificent Walker Fountain that stood in front of the Town Hall. This was given to the town by the Walker family in 1899 and a silver replica is to be found in the Town Hall.

The simple and dignified obelisk that stands by Warrington Bridge is a fitting memorial to the Warrington men who died in the two World Wars. The felspar-flecked, white stone is inscribed with the words, 'TO OUR GLORIOUS DEAD', below the bronze sword of a crusader, while the gold-hued tablets on the rounded wall behind name over 1100 Warringtonians who died in the First World War, and 442 who gave their lives in the Second. Nearby, a recently-erected tablet by The Burma Star Association (Warrington Branch) honours those who died in the Far East between 1941 and 1945.

The Cannon, Warrington

The Arpley Cannons - relics of the Crimea - sacrificed for armaments in World War II.

At the southern entrance to the town stands this striking memorial to the Warrington men who died in the two World Wars.
A.E. Howell

THE BURMA STAR ASSOCIATION
Warrington Branch

To honour those who laid down their lives in the war in the Far East 1941-45

They shall not grow old, as we that are left grow old:
Age shall not weary them, nor the years condemn.
At the going down of the sun and in the morning
We will remember them.

To commemorate the men and women who served with them in that war.

When you go home tell them of us and say
"For your tomorrow we gave our today"
~ Kohima Epitaph ~

Dedicated by their comrades-30 August 1987

`We will remember them.'.
A.E. Howell

17

Arthur Crosfield, the Whig (Liberal) who ousted Robert Pierpoint from office in 1906.

Whigs and Tories

In 1832 Warrington elected its first MP and, for many years, the loyalties of the town's electors swung backwards and forwards between the Whigs (the Liberals) and the Tories. Sir Gilbert Greenall was a very popular Conservative MP for Warrington for many years from the middle of the 19th century.

He was ousted between 1892 and 1905 by Robert Pierpoint, who came from an old Warrington family. His family home was 'The Stone House', the oldest building still standing in St. Austin's Lane. It was a gift from him to the British Legion and has been used as their headquarters ever since.

It was not until 1918 that Warrington had its first Labour candidate, Isaac Brassington, but the first contender actually to win the seat for Labour was Mr C. Dukes (later Lord Dukeston) who did so for the first time in 1923.

Since 1945, Warrington has always been a Labour town, and perhaps one of its best known MPs was Dr Edith Summerskill, a medical practitioner, opponent of boxing, and Minister of Health for a time. She represented Warrington in Parliament between 1955 and 1960.

Robert Pierpoint, Tory MP for Warrington (1892-1906), whose family home was the Stone House in St Austin's Lane.

Chapter 2: Industry

Made in Warrington

Since early times Warrington has been a town noted for the diversity of its industry. Veratinum, the Roman settlement at Wilderspool, left behind traces of much industrial activity, finds showing that considerable ore-smelting, the fashioning of jewellery and pottery, and glass-making took place. In fact, the earliest glass furnaces in Britain have been found there.

In Tudor times there was trading in flax, hemp and linen, and another early industry in the town was a fishery at Sankey Brook, and later Sankey Water Mill operated in the same area.

Warrington was also well known in times past for the manufacture of sail-cloth, and this strong material was even exported abroad via Liverpool. More than half the sails which carried Nelson's ships to victory are supposed to have been made in Warrington.

Fustian cutting was a cottage industry much practised in Warrington at one time. There is a row of three storey terraced cottages at Lymm with an outside staircase (now leading to a

The old pin mill in Latchford was pulled down in December 1907

photographic studio) which the fustian workers used to reach the long workroom that ran along the length of the third floor. There, long bales of a velvet material would be laid out along trestle tables and the women employed would use a sharp knife to cut the loops on the surface of it.

In the 16th century the Dallam family from Dallam were famous for organ building, Queen Elizabeth I commissioning an organ to be made at Dallam which was then shipped to Turkey.

Pins. Warrington was noted for its pin making as far back as the time of the Civil War. This industry expanded in the 17th century at Pinner's Brow, and child labour was often used. Greedy employers found that the nimble fingers of children could do the fiddly jobs of heading and sharpening with ease.

In 1841 an entry in Beamont's diary describes the working day of a ten-year-old Warrington boy employed at pin-heading in a local factory:

'He went to his work at half-past five each morning, and with an allowance of ten minutes for breakfast, half-an-hour for dinner, and ten minutes for tea ... continued at it until eight in the evening, nearly fifteen hours a day, and for that his wages were two shillings a week.'

The phrase 'working for pin money' probably originates from this time, when husbands gave their wives money to buy new pins from the pedlar, who perhaps only called once a year.

Tanning. In the 1930s Warrington was one of the largest tanning centres in the country with about a score of tanneries in the town, most of which were centred around Howley and Latchford. There is even written evidence of a tanyard in Tanners Lane as early as 1772.

There were few houses built down-wind of a tannery because of the awful smell. Yet the industry was still thriving in Warrington in 1947, and by then the town was particularly noted for the manufacture of industrial belting and shoe soles. The last tannery to close down was Thomas Whittle's on Mersey Street.

Parr's Bank was the first bank to be established in Warrington. It began trading in September 1788 when it was run by three partners, one of whom was Joseph Parr. Edward Greenall, founder of the local Brewery, joined the Board in 1819; his son, Peter, married Eleanor Pilkington, of Pilkington's Glassworks in St. Helens, and so began the Bank's long association with the two firms, which helped it to weather years when trading conditions were bad.

Today, Parr's Bank is the Winwick Street branch of the National Westminster. The present building, its grand banking hall crowned by a magnificent blue and gold ceiling, dates from 1877, and the words 'Old Bank' are still set into the ornate stonework over the door.

When **Bank Quay** was first developed as an industrial site it was separated from the town by green fields, known as Bank Fields, where local people would stroll, perhaps venturing as far as Arpley and Howley Meadows.

In 1698, Thomas Patten, one of the large landowners in Warrington then, was responsible

Penketh tannery, once a thriving concern, now lies derelict amid overgrown grassland.
A.E. Howell

Once Parr's Bank - the first to be established in Warrington. Now this striking building houses the Winwick Street branch of the Nat. West.

The River Mersey, an invaluable asset for the industry at Bank Quay.
A.E. Howell

for making the River Mersey navigable as far as Bank Quay at his own expense. And so the port of the town was established here, with the River Mersey providing easy access to Liverpool, and unlimited water for steam. Later, the railway was built adjacent to the works for speedier distribution of raw materials and products.

This same Thomas Patten (father of the Thomas Patten who built the Town Hall) established his copper smelting business at Bank Quay in 1717 using ore from Alderley Edge at first. Then, when that supply dwindled, ore from Cornwall and Anglesey was imported cheaply by water. Slag from his copper works was used in the foundations of the Town Hall but, by the 1820s, these copper works had disappeared.

Glassworks were also established at Bank Quay in 1750 by Robert Patten, son of another branch of the Patten family, who leased land there and manufactured court and crown glass, examples of which can be found in the Museum. There was also a cotton mill at Bank Quay at one time, and the flour mill founded by James Fairclough still flourishes.

Industrial Revolution

Many industrial firms started up in Warrington at the time of the Industrial Revolution, several of which are still thriving in the town today.

Soap. Joseph Crosfield founded his famous soap works at Bank Quay in 1814 when he was only 22. In May of that year George Crosfield, his father, wrote in his journal,

'I left Lancaster on my way to Warrington; rested at night at Yarrow Bridge - a comfortable house in a rural situation; reached Warrington next day. The object of my journey was to view some premises near Bank Quay suitable for a soapery, which business our son, Joseph, seems to have a strong inclination for.'

Joseph Crosfield believed in living near his works and resided for many years in White Cross House, which once stood on the site of Sacred Heart RC church.

The works flourished, at first producing hard soap for the domestic market and soft soap for the Lancashire textile industry. Then, under John and George, sons of Joseph, the firm linked up with Brunner Mond at Northwich, and the chemical side of the works developed. This led to a branch factory on the south bank of the Mersey being established in 1904. In 1911, during a slump in the soap trade, Brunner Mond absorbed Crosfields, and the firm was then sold to Lever Brothers in 1919, and has traded as Unilever since 1929.

However, there is still a great divide between the two facets, dating from when William Hesketh Lever (the first Viscount Leverhulme) was a great rival to Crosfield, leasing his first soapworks in Warrington, between 1886 and 1888, before moving to Port Sunlight. At War-

Crosfield's to Unilever - Perfection Soap to Persil.
E.F. Kemp

Old and new plants established on an extensive Roman site by Greenall Whitley.
A.E. Howell

23

rington, he perfected his famous 'Sunlight' soap, and lived at a house in Palmyra Square, where Forshaw Richmond (Solicitors) now practise, and where a plaque can be seen.

Several of the products manufactured at Crosfield's are well known household names. The firm produced its first dry soap powder in 1896, and the washing powder, Persil, came on the market in 1909, although the early powder had to be mixed to a paste by the housewife. The firm still continues to be a market leader with this product, and with Domestos, which is also produced at the Warrington works.

Brewing. In the 16th century only people who took in travellers were allowed to sell ale, and two centuries later beer was still only brewed at the inns established in the town to sell to their customers. So it was well into the 18th century when Greenall Whitley set up their commercial concern, with Tetley Walker and the smaller brewery at Burtonwood not far behind.

Greenall Whitley, a family-based enterprise, was set up in St. Helens by Thomas Greenall in 1762, expanding to Warrington in 1786, and to Liverpool for a short time. The original brewhouse in the town was at the Saracen's Head, on Wilderspool Causeway, but this became inadequate for the needs of the business and, in 1791, a decision was taken to erect a new, larger brewery across the road, which was completed in 1793.

Thomas had three sons to whom he left his breweries, Edward, William and Peter. The latter managed the St Helens brewery and married into the Pilkington family there. In the next generation, Edward's son, Gilbert, brought three of his nephews from the Whitley side of the family into the business - hence the name Greenall Whitley. He also became MP for Warrington for many years from 1847. His twin brother married into the Lyons family of Appleton Hall and became Rector of Stretton from 1831 to 1867, while his brother John went into banking and was closely involved with Parr's Bank.

From 1864 Greenall's also had a distillery behind Bridge Street. Here, the branded product Warrington Dry Gin was developed, and wines and spirits were sold from a shop front in Bridge Street (near Macdonalds').

During the First World War the brewery's delivery wagons were used to transport ammunition to the local railway stations for onward transmission to the battle fields. And, in 1951, Festival Pale Ale was first produced at the Wilderspool brewery - to commemorate the Festival of Britain.

In 1954 Greenall Whitley purchased a company based in Ruthin which sold table water. (The premises of this firm were built on an artesian well, noted for the purity and healing qualities of its water.) And so Cambrian Soft Drinks were developed.

For many years the premises behind Bridge Street had been very congested for the size of the operation, and eventually a new distillery and warehousing complex was developed in Loushers Lane on the fields where the brewery dray horses used to graze. The foundation stone for the new distillery was laid in 1962 and this plant gave room for expansion so that Warrington Dry Gin and Vladivar Vodka (first marketed in 1965) could enter the overseas market.

During the 1970s Grunhalle Lager was developed and, in October 1977, the modern Steinecker Brewhouse was opened adjoining the old premises on Wilderspool Causeway. This completed a brewery complex known for its 'great versatility, operational economy and high volume output'.

Tetley Walker. In 1846 Walker's Brewery was established by Peter Walker and his father in King Street. This soon moved to premises in Dallam Lane which, by the 1950s, had become one of the largest breweries in Europe. A new brewery was opened in 1967 in Gee Street costing £3m, with the layout of the plant, brewhouse and fermenting building designed by the staff. Brewing was controlled by means of a 59 foot, illuminated panel and, at that time, Tetley Walkers' was producing 20,000 barrels (six million pints) of beer a week. Since then Tetley Walker have joined with other firms to form the large consortium known as Allied Breweries.

Burtonwood Brewery dates from 1867 when it traded with free houses and local farmers. By 1907 it was producing 200 barrels of beer a week, and now the company owns about 300 pubs in Lancashire, Cheshire, Staffordshire and North Wales.

Tool Making originally started up in Warrington in the Middle Ages as a cottage industry, and has continued in the town ever since. Peter Stubs began his working life as a publican, and was the landlord of The White Bear in Bridge Street when he began his file-making industry as a sideline. His first factory was in Scotland Road, and files made there were always stamped with the initials PS - the firm's trademark.

Peter Stubs himself, however, also continued to operate as a brewer, even building two kilns for converting barley into malt. His beer was popular throughout the Manchester and Liverpool areas, and was even exported beyond the region by canal.

Later, he moved his file making business to its present base on Wilderspool Causeway, and was the first person in the area to build houses for his workers, although these were very squalid by today's standards.

Wire manufacture in Warrington has a long-standing, world-wide reputation - upheld by such firms as Rylands-Whitecross, Greenings, Lockers, and British Aluminium.

Rylands-Whitecross. John Rylands, in partnership with Nathaniel Greening, the son of a wandering preacher, set up his wire making firm in Church Street in 1810. However, Greening soon branched out on his own, and it was the far-sightedness and hard work of John Rylands' much respected son, Peter, that was mainly responsible for making the company the leading wire manufacturing firm in Great Britain by the 1950s. As a tribute to him a plaque was unveiled at the Whitecross Works in December 1949, and another one is to be found in the parish church.

The firm also produces an enormous quantity of nails for the British Market. In 1956 its machines, which punch the heads on the nails, were capable of producing 100 tons of nails every eight hours.

In 1864 the **Whitecross Wire Company** was founded by F. Monks at Bank Quay. It was built near the site of an ancient white cross that once stood on the road between Warrington and Sankey. The goods made there were sold throughout the world and all bore the emblem of a white cross. Later, the firm built its own foundry in Bewsey Road.

Although the firms of Rylands and Whitecross had been closely associated with each other for over 100 years, they only began trading under the joint title of Rylands-Whitecross in April 1970. In the 1970's, when they were producing approximately 4,000 tons of wire per week and had a 22% share of the market, they were thought to be the largest single company in the British wire industry.

Nowadays, stress relieved wire for use in concrete buildings and bridges is one of their products much in demand. The pre-stressed concrete wire for Thelwall viaduct came from their factory, and they have established world-wide markets trading in countries as disparate as Brazil and Norway.

Printing. Warrington was fortunate to have a famous printing firm operating in the town during the last half of the 18th century. William Eyres produced Warrington's first newspaper, *The Warrington Advertiser*, by hand in 1756 and, among other famous works, Eyres' Press printed Joseph Priestley's *'History of Electricity'* and *'The State of the Prisons in England and Wales'* by John Howard, the prison reformer. While this was being completed he lodged at a silversmith's shop which stood on the site of Boots, in Bridge Street, which a plaque, erected in 1906, still commemorates, together with writing in the ornate stonework above.

Alexander Mackie & Company began printing *The Warrington Guardian* in 1853 and, when celebrating its centenary, it was said to be a 'happy place to work', where news items were only accepted if they were 'accurate, fair and kind'. By then over 100,000 families took the paper and there were 16 weekly newspapers in the series, each covering a different local area.

There was a hiccup in this happy state of affairs in 1959 when a strike in the printing industry put a stop to the production of the *Guardian* for several weeks during the summer.

A happier talking point is a 'Talking Newspaper' for the Blind which was begun in 1978, and consists of a summary of the week's local news supplied by the *Warrington Guardian*, put on tape by volunteers and delivered free by the Royal Mail.

When the entrepreneur Eddie Shah bought out the paper, based in Sankey Street, in the 1980's he rented the modernised Academy buildings at Bridge Foot, and revolutionised the

Opposite:
Tablet commemorating John Howard, who lodged on Bridge Street while completing *'The State of the Prisons in England in Wales'*.

printing process with the installation of modern technology. Thus, one might say, he continued the Academy's tradition as a pioneer. To complete the picture to date, the *Warrington Guardian* series has now been sold to Reed Northern Newspapers of St. Helens.

Other Industry ... By 1787, Peel's cotton spinning factory at Latchford was using the first steam engine to be employed in the industry.

At one time Warrington had 16 cotton mills. Cockhedge Mill was the last to close in 1962 because of the import of cheap textiles, the buildings being demolished in 1983 to make way for the Cockhedge Shopping Centre.

Dallam Forge, opened in 1840, provided iron for use in the wire industry.

In 1872 the firm of Naylor's was established as a sawmill and importer of softwood timber. The home of the founder still stands in Hill Top Road, Grappenhall, its name 'Rolyan' being an anagram of Naylor. Many will remember the wilful damage caused by a fire at their timber yard in 1984.

Monks Hall was founded in 1874 by Frederick Monk, who was soon joined by his brother-in-law William Hall. This iron-making business, based in Liverpool Road, was once the largest in the world. Sadly, all that now remains is the derelict ruin of the works' canteen.

The British Aluminium Company was established in 1884 with works at Bank Quay and Latchford Locks.

In 1882 the Warrington Slate Company was established as a family business in Bold Street.

The strategic position of the Richmond Works overlooking Latchford Locks on the Manchester Ship Canal.
A.E. Howell

In 1906 the Richmond Works started trading and, by 1947, had produced over a million gas cookers. They also manufactured armaments to help the war effort.

Many once saw the word GARTONS emblazoned on a warehouse roof at Arpley. Gartons Ltd was the headquarters of one of the most famous agricultural seed firms in the United Kingdom, and, in the 1950s, over half the oats grown in Great Britain came from its supplies.

Thames Board Mills were set up in 1936 as makers of folding box board (used for packaging such commodities as cornflakes). Heavily in debt, it was closed in 1983, although Thames Case, its subsidiary which manufactures fibre board cases, still thrives.

In 1977 Roberts' shoe repairing factory on Wilderspool Causeway, together with the firm's heel bar in Rylands Street, were given to the workers. However, the two shoe shops on Bridge Street and in Stockton Heath still remained as family concerns.

New Industry. The chemical firm of Laporte Industries was established on its Warrington site in 1950.

In 1965 Fiat set up their import depot for the whole of the north region, together with a service centre, on Winwick Road, where the majority of their business nowadays comes from the supplying of spare parts.

Although UKAEA (United Kingdom Atomic Energy Authority) occupied the deserted Royal Ordnance Factory at Risley after the War in 1946, they only operated on a small scale there until about 1961, when they gradually began to develop to their present size. They then attracted BNFL (British Nuclear Fuels Limited), who design fuel apparatus for power stations, and NPC (Nuclear Power Corporation), who design equipment for nuclear power stations, to set up on the same complex.

Warrrington New Town Development Corporation. One of the reasons for Warrington being chosen as a New Town in 1968 was to attract a large amount of new industry to the town, and this they have certainly achieved. In fact, this era has become known as Warrington's second Industrial Revolution.

Three large areas of derelict land, at Risley, Padgate and Burtonwood, desperately needed developing, and today new employment areas have been set up on these. Grange was the first one to be operative, followed by Birchwood, Winwick Quay, Howley (which was a joint development with the Borough), and Westbrook (housing the Gemini Centre).

Two main assets have attracted distribution industries to Warrington: the excellent motorway communications which make markets easily accessible, and the purpose-built accommodation provided by The Development Corporation. Because of this latter fact, with each unit easily adapted to suit the needs of the individual firm, a great variety of both large and small companies have been attracted to the area.

Some of the well-known firms which have established storage depots on the sites are: Marks

The Genesis Centre, Birchwood Science Park

Excellent motorway communications and purpose-built accommodation have attracted multi-national firms to the area.
WNTDC

and Spencer, Woolworth, Safeway, Rowntree Mackintosh, Allied Breweries, and New World Gas Cookers.

Many multi-national companies have also set up bases, two from America being Digital (Massachusetts) in Birchwood Science Park, and Goodyear Tyres (Ohio) at Grange; while the Japanese firm of Sanyo has a distribution base for its electrical equipment at Risley, and Nestlé, the chocolate manufacturer from Switzerland, operates at Winwick Quay.

Perhaps the following quote best sums up the part that Warrington New Town Development Corporation has had to play in the town's industrial expansion:

'The years from 1970 to 1990 have seen the most explosive period of development in Warrington's history.'

To Market, To Market ...

Warrington began its life as a market town serving the farming area around, and trading started before 1225 when markets were held twice a week, and an eight-day fair took place twice a year. The Bull's Head was built in 1685 on the probable site of the original market in Church Street.

After the Normans built the first bridge at Bridge Foot the town centre moved from Church Street and the Howley area to Market Gate, where the higher land was less likely to flood and, in 1535, John Leland described Warrington as, 'a pavid town of a prety bignes ... it is a better market than Manchester.' Praise indeed!

In 1592, a market bell was kept and goods were not allowed to be sold until it was rung. Then, by the 18th century, the town had become noted for its Wednesday market, with fish, corn, potatoes, cattle and cloth being some of the products sold.

The first written record of an annual horse fair taking place near Horsemarket Street is in 1645, and, three hundred years later, cattle markets were held in the yards of the Lion Hotel and the Norton Arms.

The old market hall was opened in 1856 behind the Barley Mow, the stalls at first being rented on a weekly basis. By 1948, the number of stalls had increased to 300 with an annual rental, and it is remembered with nostalgia by many townsfolk as a place of bustling activity with a wide variety of goods on offer. Its precincts were enlivened by colourful characters, and one of these was the old chap who played records on a trumpet-like gramophone housed in a pram.

As you went into the market down the passage by the Barley Mow you would pass Charlie Lee's oyster stall. Charlie was not only a character but a bit of a poet as well, and on his blackboard a verse would be beautifully written on some topical subject. Charlie was also a cyclist and rode with the Warrington Wheelies until he was well into his eighties.

The fish market stood in front of the Barley Mow. Its canopy is now incorporated in The Golden Square, but both the fruit and vegetable section, and the meat market, were totally demolished to make way for this development.

In July 1974 Warrington's new market was opened. It cost £1.5m and stands behind Bridge Street to the east. There is a covered pedestrian bridge from it to a multi-storey car park. This was built on the site of the Cross family's slaughter-house, where they once killed all their own meat and ran a wholesale business, the family having been butchers in Warrington market since 1860.

The imposing entrance to the old market.
Mrs J Boden

Photograph taken in 1897 - Tudor cottages in Church Street, once the centre of the town.
F.W. Knowles

Warrington Horse Fair

Horsemarket Street took its name from the horse fair which took place nearby.

This ultra-modern market, clean and spacious, has over 200 stalls with one section for fish, cheese and meat, a second for fruit and vegetables, and a third for non-perishable goods, although the sections do tend to overlap.

Many of the same families still have stalls in the fresh food part, and they tell many tales about the primitive conditions prevailing in the old market. Until late in the 1960's there was only one hot water tap in the meat section, so that stallholders would have to queue to fill their buckets. George Dearden, who has worked on his stall since 1948, also tells of the bitter winter weather when knives froze to the marble surfaces, and the only heat was from a brazier at the back of the stall.

Whereas, in the old market there used to be eight fresh fish stalls, now there are only four. One of the oldest is Alf Critchley's, established prior to 1947, when the firm had a thriving wholesale business too and even owned their own trawler!

Alf Critchley's son-in-law well remembers the old fish market. When it rained heavily the stallholders had to sit on their stalls to avoid the water underfoot which once became four feet deep. When it snowed too the prices would be covered by flakes, and his row of chickens once disappeared completely.

There was also the memorable time when a load of live eels escaped - to be discovered not just wriggling around the stalls and the floor, but scaling the steel girders to the eaves. Then there was the turkey thief who, in his panic at being pursued down Market Street, threw the bird high in the air and legged it minus his prize!

The Bull's Head in Church Street, established on the site of the old market.
A.E. Howell

33

In the fruit and vegetable area the Bates family have been established since the early years, their stall now being called The Centre Fruit Stall; while, in the retail section, there has always been fierce rivalry between Hart's and Shapiro's fabric stalls, despite the two families being inter-married.

White's rented their stall selling sports goods when the new market opened, although the family started trading in a shop in Sankey Street at the beginning of the century as a men's outfitters. The present owner still has the original telephone agreement for the Sankey Street shop, when the telephone number was 582, you paid a rental, and local calls cost nothing. How many mothers of teenage children wish that system still operated!

Despite its cleanliness and warmth, the older stallholders still miss the character and the atmosphere of the old market and lament its demise.

A Nation of Shopkeepers

The Co-operative Society started trading in Warrington in 1860, set up by members of Cairo Street Chapel. Rev. Philip Carpenter was one of the founders, and he is also remembered for finding work and relief for Irish immigrants fleeing from their impoverished country after the potato famine of the 1840s.

The co-op's first premises were rented where their Sankey Street store now stands for £21 per annum, and Frederick Monks was its first Secretary. By the 1960s it had grown enormously, with over 1000 employees, and premises throughout the district.

Garnett's Cabinet Works. We have probably all noticed the words GARNETT'S CABINET WORKS on the roof of the building behind Cairo Street Chapel. The firm produced good quality furniture there until closing down early this century. The building, dating from 1864, which is now Woolworth's, used to be its showroom.

In 1887 **Hodgkinson's** was established in Bridge Street - where Macdonald's now stands. It was a sophisticated emporium selling high-class goods from perfumes to furniture, and also advertised its high-class dressmaking and furs department. It was sold in 1962 for £300,000.

The original owner of **Edwin Allen's Art Shop,** the grandfather of Mike, bought the premises in Buttermarket Street, in 1894, from the owner of a tea warehouse. In the early days, paints and lead (for wheelwrights) were loaded onto a bicycle, and the owner set off on a Monday morning for such distant places as Crewe and Middlewich - only returning to base on Friday night. Later, as the business flourished, a salesman was employed to do this.

By 1919 the ledgers were showing accounts in the Isle of Man, the goods being taken by bicycle to Liverpool and then ferried across the Irish Sea. By that time too, window glass was being shipped from Belgium down the Mersey to Bishop's Wharf.

Photography. There have been many photographers working in Warrington over the years but one, Thomas Birtles, was commissioned by the Borough to take photographs of state visits and many major events in the town, and so, stowed away in the Museum, there is an excellent record of many Warrington scenes. Perhaps these will soon be put on display for townsfolk to enjoy. Sadly, in 1952, Birtles' Studio on Sankey Street was sold by auction after 70 years, and is now a Chinese restaurant.

Chollerton was another well-known photographer on Sankey Street earlier this century and, in 1946, three ex-RAF chaps from the south of England bought the photographic business called Lily's Studio which operated at 1 Barbauld Street. Now renamed Friar's Gate Studio, it has always specialised in wedding photography. One of the original partners tells of Carter's Cafe on Bridge Street which used to be a popular venue for wedding receptions after the War, with sometimes as many as eight occurring simultaneously. The Fir Grove at Grappenhall, Hill Cliffe Hydro at Appleton, and The Cottage at Thelwall were also popular venues.

A family group taken by Thomas Birtles in his studio on Sankey Street.

In the 1950s, when photography was still something of a novelty, the Studio operated Clubs in the local factories. Girls would pay 1/- a week for twelve weeks and would have their portrait taken in turns. The girl who collected the money would then have her picture taken free.

In 1963, when Barbauld Street was to be widened, Friar's Gate Studio moved to its present premises on Wilson Patten Street.

Golden Square. Warrington Borough Council was responsible for the Golden Square development, an attractive, pedestrianised area of the town where the old merges harmoniously with the new. This development attracted several large retail firms to the town including a much bigger Marks and Spencer's (opened in 1977), British Home Stores, C & A, and W.H. Smiths.

New Town Developments. The Forge shopping precinct in Stockton Heath was the first Warrington Development Corporation shopping scheme to be completed. It was opened in September 1974. This attractive pedestrian precinct features three pieces of old machinery - a rolling mill, a cutter and a lathe - used originally to manufacture spades and tools of high quality at Caldwells' Forge, which was once based there. Many of the implements it produced were used in the construction of the Manchester Ship Canal.

The Cockhedge Centre has attracted superstores such as Asda, Comet and B & Q. It is appropriate that Carpetland trades there too as a cotton factory dominated the area from 1831, which concentrated on spinning yarns for tufted carpets before turning to weaving man-made fibres for dress materials.

To complete the picture, Sainsbury's has a popular superstore near the parish church, and Texas operates near Bridge Foot. Farther out of town there is the Birchwood Centre which was opened by the Development Corporation in 1980, and the Swedish store IKEA has set up its first base in Britain at the Gemini Centre, while, more recently in this area, Gulliver's World and Smith's Do-It-All are trading.

Saturday morning in the New Town shopping centre, Birchwood. *WNTDC*

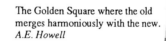

The Golden Square where the old merges harmoniously with the new. *A.E. Howell*

Machinery used at Caldwell's Forge, once sited on the shopping precinct in Stockton Heath. *Jack Gregory*

Taken in 1897, Mr Gill's butcher's shop on Higher Bridge Street was reputed to be the oldest in England.
James Harding

Snips From Past and Present

Singleton and Stephenson, once trading on Bridge Street, was supposed to be the oldest established butcher's shop in England.

J. Geddes & Son Ltd were wholesale tea and coffee merchants in Market Street, where they also had a coffee shop. Alas, the business closed in 1971 to make way for the Golden Square development.

Edward Greenhalgh & Son started off as cabinet makers from 1911. They then specialised in designing and supplying kitchens and bathrooms, fireplaces and central heating, both to the trade and the public.

Henry Millings, the well-known grocers, was sold in 1962.

Ralph (Rafe) Johnson once sold mahogany furniture in Bridge Street, and his pieces are still treasured by old Warringtonians.

There were once several clog manufacturers in the town, including Cloggy Gandy, who had a shop on the corner of Rose and Crown Street (off Mersey Street).

Broadbents had a large department store of ladies-wear on Bridge Street for many years, and now carry on the business in Stockton Heath and Knutsford.

Chapter 3: Public Services

The Three Rs

Warrington Grammar School was founded in 1526, provision of 500 gold marks for its maintenance being left in the will of Sir Thomas le Boteler, 15th Baron. It was one of the first schools to open in Warrington and, although at first free, it had a strict rule that both boys and teachers were practising Anglicans. During its early years it was housed in an imposing building in Back (Bag) Lane, with a schoolmaster's house attached. This area is now known as School Brow and the old building can still be seen behind Sainsbury's. Alas, it is but a shadow of its former self, being used as a storage depot for the Borough Surveyor's department.

In 1937 the Boteler School moved to Latchford where it opened with 500 boys and, since the comprehensive system of education became rampant throughout the country, the school has joined with Richard Fairclough Secondary Modern to become the Sir Thomas Boteler High School.

The old buildings of the first Boteler Grammar School on School Brow.
A.E. Howell

39

The Sir Thomas Boteler High School

Many children of wealthier families started their education at a Dame's School, perhaps later attending Boteler Grammar School. There were also several Charity Schools established in Warrington in the 18th century, providing education for the poorer children of the working-class. The best known is perhaps the Blue Coat School, established in 1711. It was the first school in Warrington to have a uniform and its name was derived from this.

Unfortunately, it is best remembered for its exposure, in 1868, by Dr James Kendrick, the Medical Officer of Health at the time. He revealed that the school was providing poor food, inadequate clothing and meting out severe punishments. New socks were only given out three times a year and the old ones were not washed in between(!), the girls spent over half their time making and mending clothes, and many children had fleas, worms and headlice. Not surprisingly, it closed soon afterwards.

During the 19th century religious denominations developed their own Sunday Schools and Day Schools. One of the earliest was The National School in Church Street which was opened in 1833 by the Anglicans. It had over 500 pupils on roll, each paying 1d per day. Other schools were soon opened by Nonconformists, and then, later in the century, by the Catholics.

After 1902 the Education Act, known as the Balfour Act, came into existence to promote education for all. This was closely followed by the establishment of Warrington Local Education Authority in 1903. Soon after this several 'council' schools were built, the first being

All girls together in a class at Bolton Council School in the early 1900s

Beamont in 1907, then Bolton Council School, Evelyn Street, and Oakwood Avenue.

Soon, most children received free elementary education from five to fourteen and a spate of schools were built. Bewsey had both its primary and secondary schools by 1935, and Richard Fairclough was also built by then. The Secondary schools serving the area south of the Ship Canal, however, were not in evidence until the middle of the 20th century, Appleton Grammar being the last to open in 1968. Since then many have amalgamated with their near neighbours to become one school, for example, at Lymm, and, more recently, the merger of Stockton Heath and Appleton to form Bridgewater High School in 1987.

The Academy. As one enters the town from the south one can't fail to notice the fine Georgian buildings at Bridge Foot. The Academy came into existence here as a place of education for the sons of Nonconformists, one being John Wedgwood, son of the famous potter, Josiah. It was founded in 1757, when the banks of the Mersey were willow-lined and occupied by salmon fishers. Rev John Seddon, minister at Sankey Street Presbyterian Chapel, was instrumental in the setting up of this new Academy at Warrington, and in its early success.

Warrington Academy laid the foundation for Nonconformist higher education in the town, the wide variety of subjects taught paving the way for the diverse curriculum used in schools today. The Academy also employed foreign tutors to teach languages, just as 'assistants' now do from France and Germany. For a short time, Marat, the French revolutionary, was one of these.

Joseph Priestley is the Academy's most famous tutor. He was an excellent teacher, having the foresight to introduce History into the timetable, after which it soon became an acknowledged subject on the syllabus in many other places, not least Cambridge.

He was very interested in Science and, while at Warrington, was determined to improve his knowledge of Chemistry, setting up a laboratory in a separate building behind his house in Academy Place. Physics too fascinated him and, also while at Warrington, he began his experiments with air, which eventually led to his isolation of oxygen about seven years later. The isolation of ammonia and invention of soda water can also be attributed to him.

A statue of Priestley performing an experiment, although originally unveiled in the Technical College in Palmyra Square in 1913, now stands, appropriately enough, in Priestley Sixth Form College.

Anna Laetitia Aikin (later Mrs Barbauld), daughter of one of the tutors, was probably the first person to write books for children. These were published by Eyre's Press and proved very popular. While she grew up in the town she lived in the building that now houses the Warrington Conservative Club in Buttermarket Street. Here, the pretty, white-painted iron gates have a plaque to her memory. Barbauld Street is also named after her.

It seemed possible, at one time, that Warrington Academy would become the first red-brick

THE WARRINGTON ACADEMY WAS ESTABLISHED IN THIS BUILDING IN 1757 REMOVING TO LARGER PREMISES IN WHAT IS NOW ACADEMY STREET IN 1762

This Tablet was erected in 1902 by The Warrington Society

The larger premises proved to be costly - one of the reasons for its closure in 1786.
A.E. Howell

university. However, the combination of poor discipline and bad management (which included the expensive removal to Academy Place) eventually led to its untimely closure in 1786.

Its academic tradition was upheld, in a small way, by the many societies that first met in the Academy at Bridge Foot. The citizens of Warrington owe a particular debt of gratitude to the Warrington Society, a gentleman's club housed in the Academy, which erected many plaques describing special events and buildings in the town's history.

During 1978, far-sighted members of the town's societies tenaciously fought to save the Academy from demolition. By then it had fallen into a bad state of decay and was obstructing the new road system at Bridge Foot. Eventually, word came from Whitehall that it was to be preserved as a listed building, and it was rolled 20 metres up Bridge Street to the prominent site on which it stands today.

In a way the Academy has come full circle, as its buildings have once again housed a pioneer. Eddie Shah's far-sighted use of new technology has revolutionised the newspaper industry and, hopefully, his business will not share the short-lived success of the Academy itself.

During the 19th century other educational establishments were being evolved for the older age groups. The Mechanics Institute, formed in 1824 in Foundry Street, was the fore-runner of the School of Art, which acquired premises in Museum Street in 1884, where it is still housed. Several famous artists have been students there, including Sir Luke Fildes (who illustrated the works of Dickens), Oswald Gartside, Henry Woods, and John Wood - the sculptor.

In 1891 the Technical Institute was founded, using the majestic Victorian building in Palmyra Square from 1902 to 1969 and, although this now houses the Borough Treasurer's department, its name is still carved in sandstone above the portico, together with the names of famous scientists and philosophers, not least Joseph Priestley.

The 'Tech' eventually moved to purpose-built premises on Winwick Road which were finally completed in 1974. Here, the main building is on stilts with car parking under its belly. It was evacuated for a time when it was feared a local earth tremor had made it unsafe but, happily, the fear was groundless.

Padgate Training College was established at Fearnhead, on land which had been first a racecourse, then a golf course and, finally, part of an RAF camp during the Second World War. After this, it became established as an Emergency Training College and, in 1949, became a full College of Education. Since then, it has joined with the College of Art and the 'Tech' to become North Cheshire College.

A photograph taken in 1899 of the Plague House in Wash Lane, Latchford.
Henry Bond

Photograph taken in 1902 when rubbish was still emptied onto the street.
K.F. Bishop

Health and Hospitals

Between the years 1645 and 1647 plague swept through the town, and the Plague House built at that time in Latchford was demolished only recently. It is believed that people who died of plague there were hurriedly buried in the field next door, where bones have been discovered.

From the 18th century and before, there are horrific accounts of the all-pervading stench of open sewers and food left to rot in the putrid streets of Warrington, the narrow cobbled streets in the town centre even having an open ditch down the middle for rubbish. The houses too were overcrowded and dirty, several families often sharing one outside 'privy' until the middle of the 20th century, which was when night soil carts also became a thing of the past. With these appalling conditions, it was not surprising that the town was a prey to sickness and disease.

A workhouse had been founded in the town in 1730 in Church Street, where the aged poor and destitute could live and perhaps do some menial work. An offshoot of this was a smaller workhouse set up on the corner of Mersey Street and Church Street in 1801, with a small infirmary behind.

However, as these could not cope with all the sick as well as the needy, and to counteract the spread of disease; a dispensary was set up in Market Street in 1810 - the town's first health centre. Later, it moved to a white house, which still stands next to the presbytery of St. Mary's RC church on Buttermarket Street. Later, this building became a convent, and is now about to be turned into offices.

The dispensary catered for outpatients, and those who needed beds were treated at a large house in Orford Street, where the rooms were turned into wards. By 1819 a Ladies Charity had also been set up to distribute maternity relief to the poor.

In the early years of the 19th century sanitation in the town was appalling and, in 1831 and 1832, cholera was rife, particularly in the low-lying areas around Mersey Street and Lower Bank Street. A fever hospital was eventually set up to cope with this alongside the main workhouse.

Warrington Infirmary opened in 1877, taking over from the dispensary. It was situated in Kendrick Street, which is named after Dr. James Kendrick, one of the first doctors appointed to work at the dispensary, and whose large collection of medical books is now preserved in America. The Infirmary was enlarged later from 40 to 100 beds, but was finally closed in January 1980.

In 1940 Sir Peter Rylands gave Thelwall Grange, once the Rylands' family home, to the Infirmary to be used as a convalescent home, giving people a chance to recover from illness in relative peace and quiet. And, in 1944, Hill Crest on Balmoral Road, Grappenhall, was also bequeathed to the hospital by Reuben Higham, a tanner, to be used as a nurses' home.

In 1879 an asylum was built at Winwick, which was used as a military hospital during both the World Wars, when it was known as the Lord Derby Hospital. In the First World War it was said to be the largest temporary hospital in England, looking after 6,000 men injured at the Front. Afterwards, it reverted to its sole role of caring for those suffering from mental illness. Raddon Court in Latchford was also used as a Red Cross hospital during the First World War.

1930 brought the Borough General Hospital with its own nurses' home and administrative block and, two years later, the addition of a casualty ward. In 1973, the ambulance station in Farrel Street was opened and, a year later, the Borough General was partially knocked down to make way for new extensions costing well over £14m. These were finally completed in 1980 when Phase A of the new Warrington General was opened. This massive complex provides a comprehensive range of services, and attempts to satisfy all the needs of a large, densely-populated community.

Many Warrington citizens entered the world in Victoria Park Maternity Home, an offshoot of the Borough General Hospital, and only closed when the maternity wing there was expanded. It is often referred to by its former name 'Old Warps', which originated from the Old English word 'ollerwarpe' meaning 'land built up by the deposit of silt' - probably from the bed of the River Mersey.

It is fitting to end this section by mentioning St. Rocco's hospice in Orford, which offers those suffering from a terminal illness an atmosphere of caring peace and tranquillity where they can end their days with dignity.

The "Lord Derby" Military Hospital, Winwick.

When Winwick Hospital cared for the injured in both World Wars, it was probably the largest temporary hospital in England.

Urchins wrestling in Dallam Lane in 1902.
K.F. Bishop

Books and Bygones

William Eyres, the local printer, was the first librarian of the Warrington Circulating Library, which loaned books from a specially adapted cart as early as 1760. Almost a century later, Warrington had become the first rate-aided library in England, and the present building, housing both library and museum, was opened in 1857 having been built for £2,000. A small art gallery was later added to the museum and, by the end of the 19th century, the services of the library were free to the public.

Law and Order

Warrington's first Police Force was established in 1838, and consisted of one constable and four assistants. Twenty years later the force had only grown to a chief constable and nine 'bobbies'. Firms too at this time would pay watchmen a fee to safeguard their premises and, as they patrolled the town, these men would call out the time and the weather. The Bridewell, in Irlam Street, was the town's first prison and police station but, in 1901, a new headquarters was built in Arpley Street which also houses the Coroner's Court.

Was this man in trouble at Market Gate in 1902?.
K.F. Bishop

Opposite: Photograph taken in 1897 on the corner of Rylands Street and Bridge Street.
James Harding

48

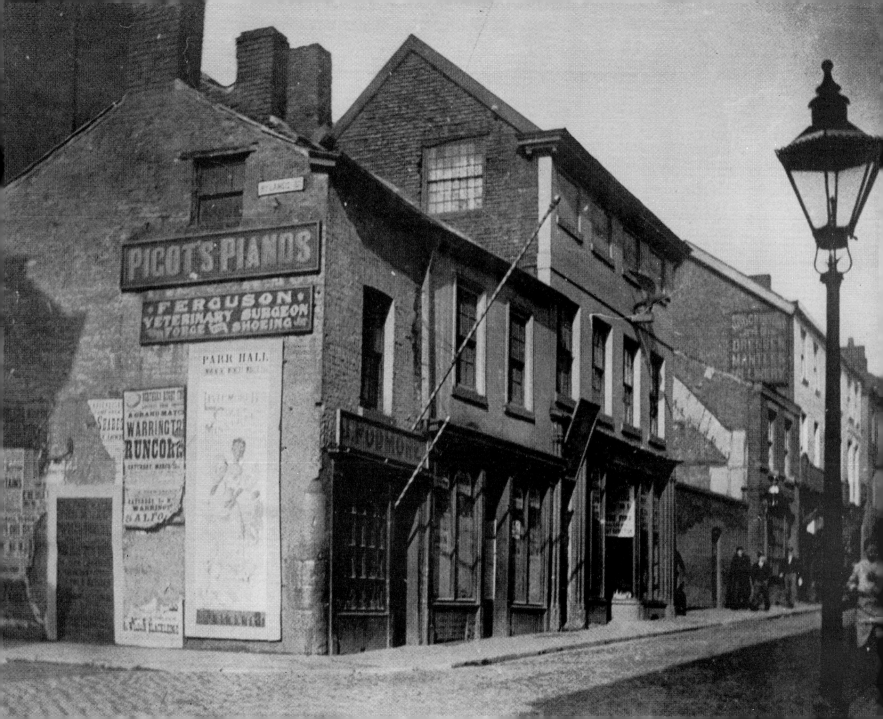

In 1969 the Warrington Borough Police Force merged with the Lancashire County Force, and, following the 1974 counties' reorganisation, has since been moved into the Runcorn Division of Cheshire. In 1977, Warrington Crown Court tried its first case, gaoling a man who attacked and robbed the owner of a fish and chip shop.

Fire! Fire!

Before the formation of the Fire Brigade every householder in the town *had* to keep a ladder for use in case of fire. And, before 1828, six Warrington insurance companies each maintained an engine and crew to deal with any fires at property insured by them. Eventually, the town started to set up its own fire-fighting service and, by 1868, the town possessed the largest fire pump in the country, which was aptly called 'The Nile'. Also in this year a manual fire engine was purchased.

The first Fire Brigade headquarters was set up at Heathside in 1879, and the houses nearby were occupied by firemen. The first steam fire engine was bought in 1880 and was named The Major. The first fire it tackled occurred in Academy Street in June of that year. By the time the headquarters moved to Queen Street The Brigade had six manual fire engines.

With the coming of the motor car, petrol fire engines were soon in evidence, and the Thomas Burton was purchased in 1913, fighting its first fire on Christmas Eve. The present headquarters on Winwick Road were opened in 1965, and the town's Coat of Arms, plus a stone with 'Fire Engine Station' on it, were brought from the former headquarters and put in the boundary wall.

An Englishman's Home ...

One of the reasons for Warrington becoming a 'New Town' at the end of the 1960s was the projected need to provide overspill housing for 40,000 Manchester people. Although by 1972 Manchester had decided that it did not need to re-house its workers in Warrington, 250 rented homes had by then been built at Longbarn in Padgate, and a variety of other housing, both rented and bought, had been planned.

Housing 'villages' at Oakwood, Locking Stumps and Gorse Covert were soon built, all within walking distance of local shops, schools, pubs and community facilities, and near the Birchwood Centre with its supermarkets and leisure facilities.

Snippets

Gas lights came to Warrington in 1820, and the town was converted to Natural Gas in 1975. Electricity arrived in 1900.

Award winning rented housing at Old Hall.
WNTDC

Chapter 4: Transport

By Road ...

In 1321 Warrington became the first paved town in Lancashire, the cobbled streets being paid for by tolls collected at the bridge crossing.

Wilderspool Causeway was constructed in 1624 as a means of crossing the low lying marshland to the south of the Mersey. The road was raised above the swampy ground on stone arches, and still is. Thirty-two of these lie between Warrington Bridge and Loushers Lane, and there was some consternation in the 1970s when one of them suddenly gave way and a bus partially disappeared through a hole in the road.

Before the 18th century, the main transporters of goods were pack horses, which were superseded, in the 1750s, by carriers' carts and then, as turnpike roads improved, by passenger-bearing stage coaches and mail coaches. Thus, by the middle of the 18th century Warrington had a bi-weekly stage coach service from the Red Lion (Bridge Street) to London. There was also a daily service to Manchester, Chester and Liverpool, while market coaches journeyed to Bolton, Leigh and Wigan. In 1773 the stage coach from Manchester to Liverpool, with a stop for dinner at Warrington, ran three times a week, the fare being 8/- (40p).

Privately-owned horse trams preceded the first public transport which began operating in 1902. The first route opened ran from Warrington to Latchford in April, and this was followed by the Wilderspool route to Stockton Heath in 1905. Eventually, citizens could travel on any

The Streets of Warrington as shown on the Legh Manuscript of 1465

Drawn up by Sir Peter Legh in 1465, the Legh Manuscript is an invaluable
document of the Warrington area, showing streets, fields and occupations.

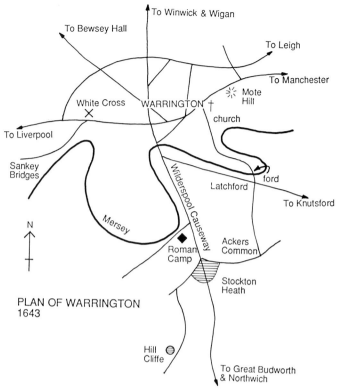

PLAN OF WARRINGTON
1643

To Winwick & Wigan
To Bewsey Hall
To Leigh
To Manchester
Mote Hill
White Cross
WARRINGTON
church
To Liverpool
Sankey Bridges
ford
Latchford
To Knutsford
N
Mersey
Wilderspool Causeway
Roman Camp
Ackers Common
Stockton Heath
Hill Cliffe
To Great Budworth & Northwich

'The first pavid town in Lancashire' - Children at play in old Church Street in 1902.
K.F. Bishop

of five electric tramway routes for a 1d fare, and the fleet comprised 21 double-decker vehicles. Trams lasted for 20 years in Warrington, by which time motor buses had taken their place. The last tram route to close, in August 1935, was the original one from Warrington to Latchford.

Corporation motor buses were purchased by the town in 1913, and their first route was a circular one to Bewsey along Lovely Lane. During both the World Wars women were recruited to act as 'clippies', and this they continued to do until January 1947. The town's new bus station replaced the former one at Arpley Street in 1978 at a cost of £2m. It provides up-to-date facilities and a covered access to the Golden Square shopping precinct.

Unfortunately, Warrington has been dogged by traffic congestion and the short-sighted planning of its road system for many years. In 1950, a Traffic Advisory Committee was formed 'to alleviate congestion' at Bridge Foot, and work was eventually started on the Barbauld Street roundabout scheme in October 1958. 1961 saw the removal of the Knutsford Road bottle-neck and, five years later, this road became a dual carriageway while, to the west, the Liverpool Road by-pass was opened in 1970.

Although Warrington is surrounded on three sides by motorways - the M62 to the north, the M6 to the east, and the M56 (completed in 1975) to the south - the town is still subject to congestion, particularly at peak hours. The plans of Warrington New Town Development Corporation have been foiled continually by the refusal of the authorities to grant permission for a north-south expressway and a new high level bridge over the Ship Canal, and it is difficult now to see any further easement of the town's traffic problems in the near future.

H.N. Houghton proudly poses in his trap on Black Bear Bridge, Knutsford Road, in 1899.
J.H. Kertland

Howley Suspension Footbridge - an attractive asset for Latchford folk.
A.E. Howell

By River . . .

River Mersey. In 1690 Thomas Patten was responsible for making the River Mersey navigable from Runcorn to Warrington, thus enabling Bank Quay to become an industrial centre and busy port.

Further upstream, Howley Quay was built in 1761, and is reputed to be the oldest up-river wharf in the North West, warehouses quickly being established along its banks. The lock at Howley Cut was built to provide access past the weir for boats going upstream. It is a good example of early civil engineering, although there was a major panic in 1948 when the weir slipped forward, placing the town's industrial water supply in jeopardy until men, working day and night, had repaired and strengthened it. Nearby, Howley suspension footbridge was opened in 1912, and has proved a great boon for those who live in Latchford and work in Warrington.

Bridge Over Troubled Waters. In the 13th century the first bridge over the Mersey was built at Bridge Foot and, when this was swept away in 1364, it was soon replaced by a second bridge. Both these structures would probably have been of wood, but the third bridge was built of stone with four arches, and was the first one to last any length of time.

Capstone from a parapet of the Victoria Bridge, built in 1837.
A.E. Howell

Opposite: Travelling south by tram along Wilderspool Causeway. The original terminus was an attractive cast iron structure outside Greenall's. The extension of theroute to Victoria Square, Stockton Heath, plus an extra penny on the fare, caused an outcry!

55

The present bridge at Bridge Foot, showing its span of eighty feet.
A.E. Howell

The Stockton Quay steps where passengers embarked en route for Manchester along the Bridgewater Canal.
Jack Gregory

It was named after the first Earl of Derby as he was responsible for its construction. He had married the mother of King Henry VII and had brought her to live at Knowsley. The king had promised to bring his queen (Elizabeth) to visit, so the Earl built the bridge to ease their journey. In fact Henry VII, in his royal carriage, was the first person to cross the bridge at the end of July 1495.

The Earl of Derby purchased the tolls on the bridge, which he then used to keep it in repair, although they were often a cause of friction for those living on the south bank. This sturdy, well-built bridge lasted for well over 200 years, and there are several inscriptions on the present bridge alluding to its importance during the Civil War.

One of these says, 'The central arches were destroyed in 1745 to check the progress of "The Young Pretender".' In fact, the bridge was rebuilt during the following year with the addition of a watch tower and a dungeon. A copper farthing dating from the 17th century, and now housed in the Museum, actually shows the tower.

The next bridge was a flimsy, wooden affair, made of one timber arch and named the Harrison Bridge after its architect. It was opened in 1813 but did not last very long.

It was followed by a stone bridge of three arches which was opened in 1837, the first year of Queen Victoria's reign, and so named after her. A capstone from one of its parapets can be seen at Bridge Foot, and a collection of coins sealed in a glass case in the stonework of this bridge can now be found in the Museum, together with a brass memorial plate.

The first half of the present bridge, and the sixth to stand upon the site at Bridge Foot, was opened by King George V and Queen Mary in July 1913. Built of reinforced concrete and, at that time, one of the widest bridges in Great Britain, it was completed two years later. Its width of 80 feet between parapets is only two feet less than Westminster Bridge in London. The strength of its structure was tested by standing five trams and two steam rollers simultaneously on the central span.

The ferro-concrete bridge at Kingsway, which takes the North-South by-pass over the Mersey, provided Warrington with its second road crossing in 1934. Then, by 1985, with the growth in road transport, the traffic at Bridge Foot was so congested that, not only was the bridge there widened, but a new bridge was also constructed upstream to make a roundabout over the river. This scheme was completed in 1987.

By Canal ...

In 1757, the Sankey Canal was not only the first still-water canal to be cut in England, but also pioneered the country's first swing bridges. Its main purpose was to transport coal from St. Helens to Warrington and, by 1771, 45,000 tons of coal was being transported annually along it.

In 1761 the Bridgewater Canal, eventually 28 miles in length, was completed as far as Stockton Heath, with James Brindley its brilliant engineer. It was originally built to distribute coal from Worsley, near Manchester, but it was soon also transporting raw cotton from Liverpool to Manchester and, by 1825, packet boats plied their wares along its length.

Stockton Quay, below the London Bridge pub in Stockton Heath, became a busy wharf, and a passenger service took people to shop in Manchester. Two of the fare stages were at Stockton Heath and Lymm, and the fare was 1d per mile!

Nowadays this pretty canal, lying to the south of Warrington, still winds through fields and woodlands, with pleasure craft chugging slowly past the as-yet unspoilt villages of Lymm, Grappenhall and Walton, while mellowed bridges and aqueducts span banks lined with fishermen and brightly coloured barges.

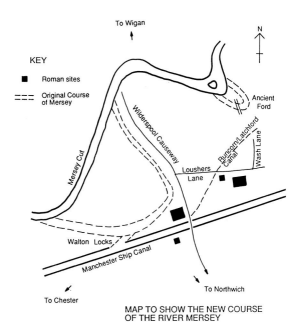

KEY

■ Roman sites

= = = Original Course of Mersey

To Wigan

N

Ancient Ford

Mersey Cut

Wilderspool Causeway

Runcorn/Latchford Canal

Wash Lane

Loushers Lane

Walton Locks

Manchester Ship Canal

To Chester

To Northwich

MAP TO SHOW THE NEW COURSE
OF THE RIVER MERSEY

A listed monument, Crosfield's Transporter Bridge - the
only one built for rail traffic.
A.E. Howell

The Manchester Ship Canal was opened in spectacular fashion by Queen Victoria in 1894 when she sailed along its entire length of 36 miles. A tremendous feat of engineering, it stretches from Eastham, where it leaves the Mersey, to Manchester.

At Warrington, the River Mersey had to be diverted in a straight cut along Chester Road to make way for it, and there is a junction of canal and river at Walton Locks. There are, in fact, five locks along its course, with those at Latchford comprising two side-by-side. One takes the largest ships plus one tug, while the narrower lock holds smaller boats.

Three swing bridges operate at Latchford, Stockton Heath and Walton, taking traffic south from Warrington. The cantilever bridge was built due to the foresight of J. Charlton Parr, who gave the Parr Hall to the Borough. Living at Grappenhall Heyes, and being a partner at Parr's Bank (now the National Westminster on Winwick Road), he visualised frequent queueing when the swing bridges were 'off'.

With the dawning of the motorway era there was the need for one structure to take the M6 over the River Mersey, the Ship Canal and the Bridgewater Canal - a tremendous feat of engineering, realised in 1963 when Thelwall Viaduct was opened.

Railways

The age of the railway came to Warrington in 1831 with the spur from Warrington to Newton-le-Willows. At that time, Warrington had three engines called 'The Warrington', 'The Newton' and 'The Vulcan', and the original station was in Dallam Lane - the Three Pigeons being the booking office.

In 1837 the Crewe to Warrington line was opened, incorporating the handsome twelve-arched viaduct at Arpley, built in red sandstone - now somewhat grimy! This line was part of the Grand Junction Railway from Birmingham to Warrington.

Three years later a passenger line from Warrington to Altrincham was completed with a station at Arpley. This line involved considerable gradient work and the building of the high level skew bridge over the Manchester Ship Canal at Latchford.

Across this line lay the notorious level crossing at Wilderspool, causing much congestion for road traffic going in and out of Warrington. The problem was solved with the completion of a bridge over the railway in May 1957, which was constructed by the local builder, Harry Fairclough. The line was eventually closed during the Beeching cuts of 1962.

Bank Quay replaced the earlier station in Dallam Lane and has been considerably altered over the years. The present Patten Arms stood where the goods depot is today and used to be the booking office. The Patten Arms Hotel itself was once a house owned by John Wilson Patten and his wife, who sold the Town Hall to the Borough. As a hotel it has always been closely connected with the railway, sometimes taking in travellers stranded in Warrington by severe snowstorms.

In 1878 Warrington Central was opened, and has been considerably modernised in recent years. Almost a century later, in 1966, the last steam train ran through this station on the Manchester-Liverpool line; while 1972 saw the electrification of the Warrington stretch of the London to Glasgow line, plus an advanced electronic signalling system.

A further phenomenon connected with rail traffic in the town is the Crosfields transporter bridge. This was used from 1916 and was the only bridge of its type built for rail traffic. It was also the last transporter bridge in the world to be constructed. Its main function was to transport single trucks from the Crosfields works on the north bank of the Mersey to the other plant on the Cheshire side. It has not been used since 1964 but still stands as a listed 'building'.

A further development in Warrington's railway system occurred when the Development Corporation opened a station at Birchwood in 1980 to facilitate rail travel between Liverpool and Manchester.

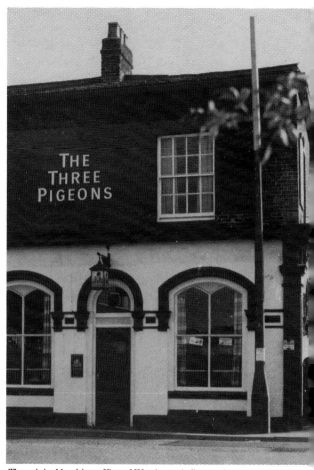

The original booking office of Warrington's first station in Dallam Lane.
Jack Gregory

Above: The vanished age of steam. This snapshot taken in April 1963 shows a train pulling into Newchurch Halt - once a station on the Wigan-Manchester line, axed in the Beeching Cuts.
Brian Neale

Below: Workmen laying bitmac carpet on the Wilderspool Crossing bridge in July 1956.

Above: Still a prominent, if decrepit, landmark; once the goods depot for Warrington Central.
A.E. Howell

Below: Crosfield's soapery towers above the functional facade of Bank Quay station.
A.E. Howell

Chapter 5: Entertainment

The Parr Hall

The Parr Hall was presented to the Borough in September 1895 by Charlton Parr, descendant of Joseph Parr who founded Parr's Bank. Last of the line, Charlton Parr himself was a partner in the bank and lived at Grappenhall Heyes.

Its magnificent organ was built in the 1870s by the master organ builder Cavaille-Coll. A national treasure, it is the only one still in existence in its original form. It was sold to Warrington Corporation in 1926 and has been used for recitals by many famous organists ever since.

Stage and Screen

Live theatre has always been popular in Warrington and, although there is no professional theatre company in the town nowadays, it is still provided by theatrical and operatic groups

The magnificent Cavaille-Coll organ in the Parr Hall. *61*
Jack Gregory

performing in such places as the Parr Hall, the Co-op Hall and Crosfields Centenary Theatre.

In May 1867, Charles Dickens visited the town to give readings from his works at the Public Hall in Rylands Street. This later became the Royal Court Theatre and was on the site of the supermarket, Lennons, which has recently closed.

Another well-remembered theatre, the Theatre Royal, sometimes called the Old Theatre, stood in Scotland Road early last century. Old playbills that have survived from then show that Mrs Siddons played there, and this playhouse was often given the nickname 'The Blood Tub' because of its partiality for gruesome melodrama!

At the beginning of this century a Music Hall opened in Friars Gate called the Palace and Hippodrome. It started as a variety theatre in 1907, then became a cinema, and for many years now has been a Bingo Hall. No one could accuse it of not moving with the times!

With the coming of film-making many cinemas sprang up all over the town, the Grand Cinema being the first and lasting until 1952. During the Second World War, and afterwards when cinemas were in their heyday the town boasted nine, and also two theatres.

There were even three cinemas in Latchford. One of these was The Premier in Powell Street, which had a performance known as the 'Tuppenny Rush' when adults paid 2d and children $^1/_2$d! In addition to this, anyone bringing bottles or jam jars for recycling was allowed a free show - the original bottle bank! Alas, this cinema was closed in 1959.

In 1921, the Empire opened in Buttermarket Street and was the town's first 'luxury' cinema, having a ten-piece orchestra, and showing the first 'talkies' in the town. Unfortunately, it was forced to close in 1961. Next door to it, the Odeon was built in 1937, and this boasted a Compton organ, a restaurant and air conditioning. One local resident remembers being taken out for lunch as a youngster in the '50s when it cost 2/- at The Empire, and 2/6 at the Ritz - where you got custard with your apple pie!

Nowadays, the Ritz at Bridge Foot, which opened in 1937, has been converted to Mr Smith's Nightclub, and the Odeon is the last remaining cinema in the town centre. Recently, however, it has had to vie with the new ten-screen cinema at Westbrook, with its free car parking facilities and American-type stalls selling popcorn and coke.

Spectrum Arena

In the 1970s Spectrum Arena was built at Birchwood by Warrington Development Corporation as a multi-purpose entertainment centre. Despite staging national snooker tournaments, playing host to the Liverpool Phil for a series of sold-out concerts, and being the venue for other prestigious events, it closed in 1986 - perhaps due to bad management?

Chapter 6: Sport

From early times Warrington has provided its citizens with a variety of sporting pursuits. Cock fighting and bear baiting were once popular, with Cock Hedge getting its name because it formed a natural arena for the former cruel practice. In the early years of the 18th century horse races proved popular at Latchford each July, while, in 1905, the town's first municipal bowling green was opened in Victoria Park, and this was followed in 1920 with tennis courts there. The town also boasts a superb athletics track in Victoria Park.

The Regatta

Rowing flourished in Warrington in the first half of the 19th century, with a regatta being held annually on the Mersey. Most races took place between Wilderspool and Warrington Bridge, with the Warrington Cup, an open race, perhaps the most popular event. Refreshment tents and entertainment booths lined the Cheshire bank, where wide-bottomed sailing boats called 'flats' were moored, providing covered grandstand seating.

By 1840, the Regatta had become part of a Warrington Sports Day, with horse racing, and other events such as catching the pig, climbing the pole, and wheelbarrow races, all taking

The Warrington Festival of 1986 heralded the revival of rowing in Warrington.
Warrington Guardian

place on Arpley Meadows. Unfortunately rowing ceased on the Mersey after 1863 because of river pollution, and in 1890 the river was diverted to make way for the Manchester Ship Canal, the old bed having now been filled in.

In recent years, a clean-up of the Mersey has resulted in a young seal being spotted in June 1951 which unfortunately had to be shot at Paddington Lock. This was followed, in July 1967, by the sighting of salmon, and, since then, with a resurgence of interest in rowing in the town Warrington Rowing Club has been reformed. The Old Quay Tavern acted as its base until the Mersey Basin Campaign stepped in with money from ICI and other firms, which enabled members to build a new boathouse near Kingsway Bridge.

Up The Wire!

Warrington Rugby Club was formed in 1879, when it rented a field almost opposite the White Hart in Sankey Street for its first season, the pub providing changing rooms and social facilities. Unfortunately, before the next season began, the Warrington Guardian had bought this land and built on it. So, after several other moves, the Wires ended up at their present club at Wilderspool.

The Wire team and the three Rugby League trophies won by them in 1954.

Rugby was curtailed somewhat during both the World Wars, but The Wire had an amazing run of success in the post-war years, winning the Lancashire League trophy in both 1948 and 1949. Then, in 1950, they beat Widnes by 19 goals to nil at Wembley to win the Rugby League Challenge Cup, which was presented to the team by the Prime Minister - Clement Attlee. The Club followed this by winning the Challenge Cup championship, the Lancashire League Cup and the Wardonia Cup in 1954.

Warrington's best Rugby season to date, however, was 1973/4 when the Club won the Rugby League Challenge Cup at Wembley under Alex Murphy, beating Featherstone Rovers 24-9. They then won the club championship, beating St. Helens 13-12 to do so (a close shave), and eventually ended up with five trophies at the end of the season.

1973/4 The team that achieved total triumph in the Wire's most successful season.
Warrington Guardian

In the Swim

Warrington public swimming baths in Legh Street were opened in 1866 and then acquired by the Council for the town in 1873 for £1,100. The town's first swimming club was founded in February 1879; the second, *The Warriors*, was formed almost a century later in 1972. Both continue to thrive and nurture fresh talent.

The old pavilion at Arpley in 1872, later replaced and used as the groundsman's hut.

In the Swing

Warrington Golf Club at Appleton came into existence in 1903, and for many years extended onto the opposite side of London Road. Atop its sloping greens is a stone obelisk surrounded by four lions - prominent landmark for miles around - which may have been erected originally as a folly on the Lyon's estate.

In 1970 Walton Municipal Golf Course was opened and has thrived well alongside its upper-class neighbour.

Warrington Sports Club

This is the oldest amateur sports club in the area. Cricket was played in the town in the middle of the 19th century, first in the grounds of the Town Hall, and then at Arpley Meadows where rabbits multiplied happily under the original pavilion. Bowling, tennis and hockey were also played at Arpley until 1968 when the club moved to Walton and became Warrington Sports Club.

Squash courts were built instead of a bowling green; and nowadays archery, darts and quiz matches have been incorporated into a busy programme. In recent years the squash section has held several major tournaments at the Club, and the cricket section regularly hosts Cheshire's minor county games. The hockey section is also strong, the men's first team playing in the National League formed in 1988.

The Cricket team at Warrington Sports Club in the 1950s.

Leisure Centres

During the last twenty years recreation centres have been set up by the Development Corporation (often with joint school use), at Broomfields, Great Sankey Forum, Woolston Leisure Centre, Padgate High School, Fordton, and the Birchwood Centre. These incorporate large, multi-purpose sports halls, swimming facilities and squash courts. In addition, Pilkington's Tennis Centre at Birchwood has four indoor tennis courts which came into use in the autumn of 1988.

Hockey 1989-style! Defensive play - not fear of an invasion from outer space!.
Mike McNamee

Chapter 7: Civic Pride

Warrington a Borough

It was in 1847 that the town of Warrington became a Corporate Borough, with William Beamont, solicitor and eminent local historian, its first Mayor. The town's population at that time was estimated at 20,000.

Town Hall

In 1750 the Patten family built Bank Hall as their family home. Standing on the edge of the town amid fields, it had an uninterrupted view over the Mersey into Cheshire. The design of the house is attributed to the architect James Gibbs and, in 1873, its purchase to be the new Town Hall cost the ratepayers £9,500. It replaced the original building at Market Gate, the facade of which can still be seen in Golden Square, which was by then too small. This magnificent Georgian mansion has been Warrington's Town Hall ever since - a building of which its citizens can be justifiably proud.

The foundations of Bank Hall are thought to be unique, as they are laid in copper slag, a waste product from Thomas Patten's copper smelting works at Bank Quay. The slag was cast into moulds and set like masonry, and evidence of this can still be seen in the cellars. The partitioning of the glass in the window frames is also much thinner than in other Georgian houses, because copper and iron from the works was used to strengthen them.

The ornate stonework in the eaves above the central door show the Arms of the Patten family, while the date of the building's completion is still visible on the side walls, carved in the stonework under the rainwater heads.

The spacious entrance hall has an imposing stone chimney-piece, various coats of arms, and a fine mosaic floor, which was put down in 1902 to replace the original wooden flooring. Italian craftsmen designed and installed it, and four sets of initials can be spotted in the design:

JWP John Wilson Patten	-	who sold Bank Hall to the Borough
TL Thomas London	-	the Borough Engineer
LW Lionel Whittle	-	the Town Clerk
QV Queen Victoria	-	who granted Warrington's Charter as a Borough in 1847

The main rooms have been carefully converted to house the town's officials adequately while still maintaining their former splendour. The council chamber used to be two rooms - the great hall and the music room - while the committee rooms were once the dining room and the ladies' retiring room, and the Mayor's Parlour was a reading room.

The facade of Warrington's first Town Hall can be seen in the Golden Square..
A.E. Howell

The splendid Georgian building that is Warrington's Town Hall today.
A.E. Howell

The buildings flanking the main hall are now offices, but once provided stabling, coach houses and accommodation for servants. When it was used as a private residence, Thomas Patten's horses grazed on the lawn in front of Bank Hall, and early photographs show a mound in front of the main building, supposedly to discourage prying eyes. Perhaps this was not enough to deter snoopers for, by the time Bank Hall was purchased by the Borough, the building was surrounded by a high wall and couldn't be seen from Sankey Street. Our magnificent Town Hall gates were originally purchased, therefore, to give the public a view of the building.

Golden Gates

In 1893 the well-known local industrialist, Frederick Monks, spotted the gates lying neglected at a foundry in Ironbridge in Shropshire where they had been cast.

There are several stories told about how these gates finally ended up in Warrington. One says that they are supposed to have been commissioned by a livery company as a gift for Queen Victoria, to be used at Sandringham which she had recently purchased for the Prince of Wales (later King Edward VII). However, when the gates were erected in Rotten Row, London, for her inspection, framed in the gateway was a statue of Oliver Cromwell to which she took offence, and so refused the gift. Sandringham's loss was Warrington's gain!

Warrington's golden gates - topped by its last four virgins!.
A.E. Howell

70

November 1955, Warrington Borough Council at work in the Council Chamber - once the great hall and music room of the Patten family home.

Another story simply says that Queen Victoria admired the gates at the London Exhibition of 1862, where they were on view before being brought to Warrington. The gates themselves were designed by John Bell, who also designed the statue of Oliver Cromwell at Bridge Foot. The four goddesses on top represent Nike, the Greek goddess of Victory. At the end of the Second World War rumour had it that these figures were Warrington's last four virgins!

Although considered one of the finest sets of gates in the country, by 1977, having weathered the north-west climate for over a century, they were badly in need of attention. All the ironwork was rusty, bits were missing, and one of the four main columns had been hit by a lorry.

The restoration work was carried out by a Buxton firm at a cost of £33,000. To add to the transformation, the four angels on top were each covered in gold leaf ('tarted up' according to one eminent historian!), and this task alone took a month to complete. Rehung in their original position fronting the Town Hall, the Queen visited Warrington in November 1979 to see them in their revitalised glory.

Mayoral Transport

1974 was the year of the new county boundaries when Widnes and Warrington were moved into Cheshire. The rates shot up nationwide and the Government eventually refunded some of the increase to the rate payers after a national outcry. In Warrington, to add insult to injury, the Borough Council wanted to purchase a second hand Rolls Royce to replace the aged Daimler. Eventually, a Ford Dorchester was bought instead at considerably less expense, and it was not until 1980 that the Borough Council was able to buy a Rolls for the Mayor. At a cost of almost £13,000 this was a 1949 Silver Wraith, although the man in the street was still not pleased!

One Hundred Years On

In 1947 the centenary celebrations took place of Warrington becoming a Borough. In the Parr Hall there was an exhibition of the town's many industries, and a pageant that took place in the same building in October proved so popular that its fortnightly run was extended by three days.

Also in that year three histories of the town were published: 'Warrington 100' by G.A. Carter, 'Warrington Ancient and Modern' by A.M. Crowe, and 'Warrington - a Heritage' by H. Boscow, all three providing an invaluable historical record of the town.

Royal Visit

In 1901 Edward VII, nick-named Edward the Peacemaker, became King. In July 1909, a year before his death, he made a royal visit to Warrington with Queen Alexandra and Princess Victoria. Although there was general disappointment when he only spent four minutes at the Town Hall, the well-known Warrington photographer Thomas Birtles, preserved the visit for posterity.

The flying visit of Edward VII in 1909 photographed by Thomas Birtles.

Chapter 8: Festivals and Fetes

The early years of the 1950s brought several national celebrations. For the Festival of Britain in 1951 the Borough staged an Industrial Exhibition at Bank Park, which was opened by Lord Derby.

June 2nd 1953 was the Coronation of Queen Elizabeth II when celebrations were held throughout the land.

1977 was the Queen's Silver Jubilee when, in June, a procession of 65 floats went from the Town Hall to Victoria Park watched by a crowd of about 20,000; and fetes, sports and street parties took place throughout the town.

Walking Day

The greatest annual occasion in Warrington is undoubtedly Walking Day. This festival was founded by the Rector of Warrington, Reverend Horace Powys, in 1835. His aim was to provide an alternative form of entertainment for the poor on 28th June when race meetings were held at Haydock and Latchford Heath. Reverend Powys was incensed at the number of parents who gambled money they could ill afford on the horses, thus causing increased hardship to their children.

The races died out before the end of the 19th century but Walking Day was, by then, well established, the procession often followed by outings into the surrounding countryside, sometimes as far afield as Frodsham. Although it was washed out for the first time in June 1928, and lapsed during the Second World War, it was re-introduced in June 1945 on a day of golden sunshine. The following year it proved as popular as ever when more than 10,000 people were involved.

Nowadays, Warrington Walking Day takes place on the last Friday in June, many schools still closing for the day. The ceremony starts with a short service followed by a procession of witness, in which most of the town's religious denominations take part. Bunting, bands and banners herald the arrival of decorated floats followed by citizens of all ages, sects and creeds, dressed in their Sunday best. As the procession wends its way through the town's streets, the spectators run out to give the children money to spend at the fair later. The rest of the day is then taken up with eating, playing organised games, and other festivities.

The surrounding villages also have their own Walking Day traditions which take place during the summer months, and Bawming the Thorn is an ancient custom associated with Appleton Thorn.

All Warrington was decorated for the Coronation of
Queen Elizabeth II on 2nd June 1953

Opposite: Buffalo Bill's Wild West Show came to
Warrington in 1903.
J.H. Kertland

Latchford Walking Day in the 1890s.

Warrington Festival

Warrington Development Corporation started and serviced the first Warrington Festival in 1972. It now takes place in May each year, providing the best from the arts and popular entertainment, as well as offering other activities provided by local societies.

Nowadays, **Warrington Horse Show and Country Fair** takes place each year on May Bank Holiday Monday at a venue south of the river (at present at Daresbury). It attracts crowds of Warrington people and, in addition to international show jumping, there is clay pigeon shooting, a tug-o'-war competition, archery, a dog show, many stalls, and Greenall's Brass Band.

Chapter 9: Parks, Gardens and Walks

The town's first public park was Bank Park which was bought for £13,000 at the same time as the Town Hall. George Crosfield, the father of Joseph who founded the soap works, donated money for its purchase, and the plaque over the door of the rather dilapidated conservatory commemorates both him and his wife.

The drinking fountain in Bank Park was erected in memory of the Rev. Philip Carpenter, once minister of Cairo Street chapel and co-founder of the Co-op Movement in Warrington. He had a great interest in shells, and emigrated to Canada in the middle of the 19th century. The formal rose garden was laid down in 1953 to commemorate the Coronation.

Queen's Gardens and Victoria Park were both bought to provide open spaces in the busy town, and to celebrate Queen Victoria's Diamond Jubilee and the 50th anniversary of the Borough.

In 1915, Alderman Arthur Bennett spearheaded the campaign for the purchase of Orford Hall and Park, which was presented to the town in memory of the Warrington men who fought in the 1914-18 War. Sadly, the hall was demolished in 1935.

Bewsey Recreation Ground was made available for public use in 1928, while to the south of the town, Walton Hall and Park was purchased in 1941 from Lord Daresbury for £19,000. A large part of the parkland and all the greenhouses were devoted to food production during the last War; and nowadays it provides many recreational facilities for the local people, and the display of rhodendrons in late spring is magnificent.

Woolston Park Jubilee Garden was opened to commemorate the Silver Jubilee of Queen Elizabeth II, and was the first urban park to be built for many years.

Since its inception in 1969, and despite the fears of country lovers who felt that the little natural beauty left in the area would be eradicated, Warrington Development Corporation have provided several attractive linear parks on the outskirts of the town. Neglected land has been reclaimed, pleasant walks established, and each area is serviced by a Ranger.

Two of these areas to the south of Warrington are The Dingle at Lymm and Lumb Brook Valley on the outskirts of Stockton Heath, while to the west of the town, Sankey Valley Park stretches for 12 miles from Widnes to St. Helens. The New Town has developed about five kilometres of this on the outskirts of Warrington, and the area makes a pleasant outing for both adults and children.

The pretty wrought iron fountain in Queen's Gardens commemorates Queen Victoria's Diamond Jubilee.
A.E. Howell

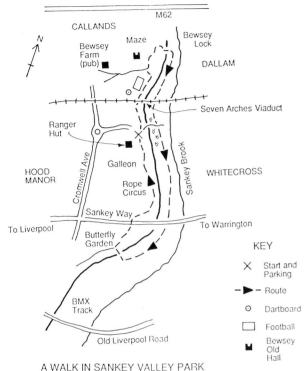

CALLANDS

A WALK IN SANKEY VALLEY PARK

KEY

✕   Start and Parking

– ▶ –   Route

○   Dartboard

▭   Football

▉   Bewsey Old Hall

A Walk in Sankey Valley Park

By Car: Take the A57 from Warrington towards Liverpool. After leaving the town turn right at the first set of traffic lights along Cromwell Avenue, and then turn right again to the car park.

Time taken: About one hour.

The rangers, based in Bewsey Hall, have informative leaflets on the canal age, local ghosts and legends, flora and fauna. Children will enjoy exploring the colourful wooden galleon or clambering over the rope circus, and there is also a BMX track and a football pitch.

For a pleasant ramble go north from the hut along the pathway to the Seven Arches viaduct which carries the busy Manchester to Liverpool railway over both the canal and Sankey Brook. Metal plates can still be seen preventing the tow ropes attached to the horses from wearing away the soft sandstone of the bridge, and the high rectangular arch above the canal once allowed the tall masts of sailing flats to pass under the viaduct.

Keep ahead past the monster dartboard (which forms an excellent children's slide), the football area and a delightful water garden, to reach the now-static, Bewsey swing bridge. Off to the left is a new pub - Bewsey Farm - which offers food, drink, and loud music! As you continue forward the massive bulk of Bewsey Old Hall appears to your left.

The original **Bewsey Hall** was a moated manor house and was built in the 13th century when the Botelers moved from Mote Hill. An account of the hall dating from then tells that it was oak framed with plaster infilling, had narrow slits for windows, a nail-studded oak door and a crenellated tower. It was also surrounded by a broad moat that could be crossed by a drawbridge. The Bewsey Hall of today is the oldest standing building in Warrington and parts of it date back to 1597. In August 1617 James I spent a night there when he knighted the owner, Thomas Ireland.

There is a gruesome tale passed down from Civil War days that tells how the owner of Bewsey Hall, then a member of the Boteler family, displeased the Earl of Derby by refusing an invitation to visit him. The Earl's followers bribed the porter of the Hall to let them in one night, whereupon they murdered the owner, and took over the house. Later, a page-boy came down the stairs with a large box supposed to contain the severed head to be put on a spike at Bridge Foot. He was allowed to pass. However, on discovering that the heir had been smuggled out in the box instead, the assassins paid the porter his gold as promised, and then strung him up on a tree for double-crossing them.

A maze stands nearby in the parkland, at the far end of which you can drop down through trees to Bewsey Lock where you cross the end of the canal and turn right along the opposite bank.

After passing under the viaduct again walk alongside a bog garden with a large duck population and, where this ends, you can bear left to double back through the feathery shade of hawthorn trees before crossing the bridge back to the car park.

Alternatively, you can continue down the bank, which takes you under Sankey Way to the next bridge. Here you can either continue to the BMX track, or simply return via the butterfly garden, rope circus and galleon.

Risley Moss - Its History

To the east of Warrington, Risley Moss is one of the last remaining areas of post-glacial mossland in the country. The Moss itself is all that remains of the raised bogs which once covered much of the Mersey Valley between Warrington and Manchester. At one time it was a raised and growing peat bog thriving above a large basin filled with soggy, rotting vegetation, that was dominated by the spongy sphagnum moss.

At the time of the Industrial Revolution a small band of hard-working farmers found the back-breaking job of clearing this land healthier than working in the factories. The peat-cutting industry too thrived here for a time. However, after the Second World War, the area was neglected and became badly overgrown.

In 1975, Warrington New Town began to develop Risley Moss with three main aims in mind - recreation for the people in the parkland, an education centre for school children and students to study both the social and the natural history of the area, and conservation of the rare and fragile mossland. The country park and nature reserve was opened by David Bellamy in 1980.

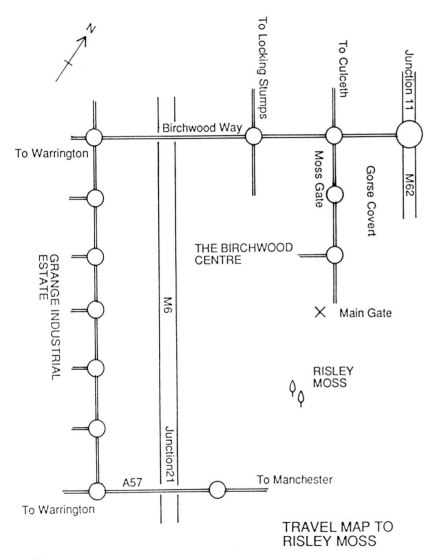

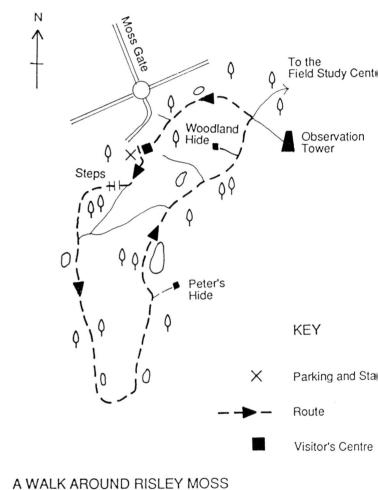

TRAVEL MAP TO RISLEY MOSS

A WALK AROUND RISLEY MOSS

KEY

✕ Parking and Sta

▶ — Route

■ Visitor's Centre

A Walk Around Risley Moss

Time taken: Under one hour.

Walk up from the car park to the Visitors Centre, itself worth a visit with its interesting displays and informative video. In front of the building turn right to pass a small pond before bearing right again down some steps where there is a display of peat cutting.

When you reach a junction turn right again and keep through woodland interspersed with ponds and glades of silver birch, each tree capable of absorbing 30 gallons of water a day. Their branches offer feathery shade as you perhaps turn aside to visit Peter's Hide or, later on, Woodland Hide.

Then return to the main path and follow the signs to the observation tower which gives a splendid view over the conserved mossland to the Pennines, with Shutlingsloe and Croker Hill prominent on a clear day. After returning to the main path, keep forward at the crossroads to return to the visitors' centre past a picnic site.

Town Trail

Time taken: About one hour.

The starting point is the town's oldest relic, the erratic left behind from the Ice Age opposite Kwik Save on Academy Street. Walk up Buttermarket Street, which probably got its name because a butter market was held in the vicinity. Notice the Odeon, the town centre's one remaining cinema and, poised on the roof opposite Edwin Allen's Art Shop, the pelican gobbling a fish - reminder of the Pelican Hotel that was once here.

You soon reach Market Gate where the four main streets of the town intersect. The town's centre was first based on Church Street, the oldest thoroughfare, but moved here onto higher ground near the bridge, and the first mention of Market Gate is in a document dated 1363. A roundabout was constructed here in 1938, which used to be bright with flower beds, and traffic lights operated from 1961 until it became the pedestrianised area it is today.

Turn left down Bridge Street, noticing the splendid, first-floor architecture. A plaque outside Boots, and carving above, denote the lodgings of John Howard, the prison reformer, and Martin's Bank used to occupy the attractive half-timbered corner building now housing the Co-op Bank.

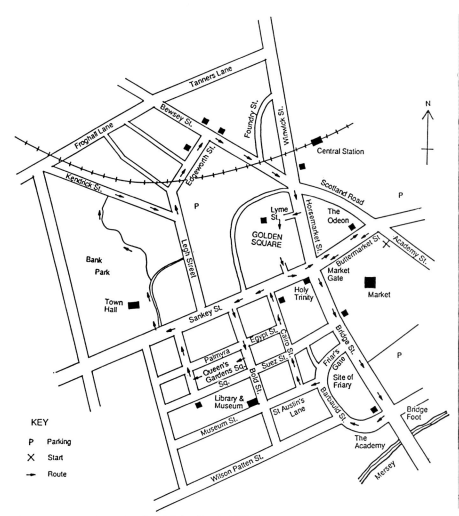

KEY

P Parking

X Start

•← Route

Opposite: Bridge Street taken from Market Gate in 1908. Changes were obviously no more popular then than they are now!

Traffic lights, floral roundabout and Boots Corner - vanished sights at Market Gate.
Mrs J. Boden

T. J. LEE
THE NOTED
IRISH LINEN SHOP
LINEN & LINEN GOODS
OF EVERY KIND

WARRINGTON
ATTLE OF OLD BRIDGE STREET: "THE LAST STAND!

Opposite is Ye Olde Lion, a coaching inn of late Stuart architecture, which boasts a stained glass window dating back to 1690, and installed when the inn was completed during the reign of William and Mary. The large courtyard at the rear once had livery stables and, possibly, a smithy.

Bridge Street, built in the 13th century as a road connecting Sankey Street and Church Street with the bridge, was originally called Newgate Street. An account of it written in 1453 says that it was very narrow and lined with timbered houses. Their overhanging upper storeys, strung with lines of washing, shut out much of the light. Its name had been changed to Bridge Street by 1580, and it was widened early in the 20th century, as also was Buttermarket Street.

Continue down to Bridge Foot, dominated by The Academy where Joseph Priestley was once a tutor, and now home of the *Warrington Guardian*. Alongside it stands the imposing bronze statue of Oliver Cromwell. You may wish to spend some time exploring the bridge and its surrounds if the traffic isn't too menacing. Tucked away on the opposite bank are Marshall Gardens, named after a Mayor and former Labour politician, who opened the Wilderspool Crossing Bridge and lived to be a centenarian.

Continue towards Mr Smith's Nightclub, passing the capstone from the earlier Victoria Bridge before turning right up Barbauld Street. Look out for the plaque telling of the friary that once stood here, before turning left into St Austin's Lane past the Postern Gate.

Ahead is 'The Stone House', the oldest building in the area, and once home of the British Legion. However, you are going to turn right up Cairo Street, passing Suez Street and Egypt Street, all named to commemorate the honours won by the South Lancashire Regiment in the Napoleonic Wars.

You soon pass Cairo Street chapel with its many memorials to local families, and the grave of the infant son of Mrs Gaskell, the 19th century novelist. Then turn left down Sankey Street, first mentioned in a deed dated 1390, and widened considerably in 1961.

Turn left again into Bold Street, and then right into Queen's Gardens to pass the O'Leary statue. On the offices of Forshaw Richmond to the left is a plaque surmounted by the head of Lord Leverhulme. Look left again, as you exit from the far end of the park, to see the building that first housed the technical college.

Next, turn right up Springfield Street and, at the top, look right down Sankey Street at the once-prestigious town houses. Bank Hall was where the steward lived when Bank House (the Town Hall) was the Patten family home. Further along, Number 84 was Holy Trinity vicarage for a short time while, set at an angle opposite, stands Holly House, once the last house before the meadows known as Bank Fields spread down to the river.

After this, turn left to walk through the 'golden gates' and up to the Georgian Town Hall with its ornate rainwater heads. Turn right in front of the building and then left alongside it, where the date of its construction can be spotted.

Continue into Bank Park where you come to the fountain dedicated to Philip Carpenter and, farther on, the sadly disintegrating conservatory leads you into Kendrick Street where you turn right to pass the site of the Infirmary. Ahead is Legh Street car park, on top of which, if you have the energy to climb there, an excellent view over the town can be obtained.

Turn left, then right into Edgeworth Street, passing Wycliffe Reform Church, and then pausing to view the former Liberal Club, dedicated to John Crosfield, one-time Mayor and son of Joseph who founded the soap works. Turn right into Bewsey Street where the Georgian terraces have been tastefully renovated in this now-peaceful street. There is a plaque on the house where Gilbert Wakefield lived when a tutor at Warrington Academy.

You soon go under the railway bridge and pass the entrance to Foundry Street where Smethurst's foundry once stood. The imposing building of Old Bank, once Parr's Bank and now the National Westminster, faces you as you reach Winwick Street. The date of 1877 is on its side and, if open, the magnificent banking hall, complete with golden candelabra, is worth seeing, before you turn alongside it past Number Three - a house considered to be the finest Georgian building in Warrington. As you pass the corner of Scotland Road notice the Theatre Tavern, near which the Theatre Royal once stood.

Continue for a short way down Horsemarket Street, which dates back to at least 1645, and was so named because an annual horse fair took place nearby. The half-timbered premises lining the street, including the printing works of Eyre's Press, were destroyed by fire early in the 19th century. Later, in 1938, the road was widened considerably and lined with the imposing buildings you see today, their first storey columns of Portland stone providing an imposing facade.

The Barley Mow - an outstanding example of Elizabethan architecture. The plaque on the building next door marks the offices of William Beamont, the town's first Mayor.
A.E. Howell

Turn right up Lyme Street to the Golden Square. The picturesque listed building on your right is the Barley Mow. Built in 1561 during the reign of Elizabeth I, it is one of the oldest examples of Tudor architecture in the town. First mentioned as an inn early in the 19th century, its name means 'heap of barley' or 'place where barley is stored'.

When built, the black and white timbered frontage would have had holes in the walls for windows, perhaps with shutters to keep out the worst of the weather. For many years glass was a luxury only the wealthy could afford, and the first panes used in pubs were composed of thick green bottled glass. Inside is a Jacobean chimney and a stuffed bear, but the 17th century staircase has disappeared.

The house next to the Barley Mow, dating from about 1780, was where William Beamont practised as a solicitor. He was the town's first Mayor and an exceptional local historian who wrote an invaluable series of books about Warrington and Cheshire.

Turn left, passing under the canopy where the fish market used to be, to reach the sculpture of the Mad Hatter's Tea Party, commemorating Lewis Carroll, son of a Daresbury vicar. Opposite this, behind the ornate fountain, is the facade of the original Town Hall, at present Ashman Studio. Two elegantly-bracketed street lamps from a bygone era have also been reproduced on this building, while the inscriptions on other gas lamps in the square show that these were made at Smethurst's foundry.

Keep ahead to Sankey Street to see the ornate stonework above Woolworths, together with its date of 1864, and the initials RG, standing for Robert Garnett - one-time owner of the furniture business here. Bear left back to Market Gate past Holy Trinity, where a hot drink or snack might be available before you return home.

This sculpture of the Mad Hatter's Tea Party enhances the Golden Square.
A.E. Howell

Fun in the 1964 floods in Liverpool Road.

Whether the Weather Be Cold ...

1949 brought a glorious summer, paid for in 1950 when every day seemed to be rainy, causing someone caustically to comment, 'The summer will be remembered by its absence.'

July 1964 brought a great storm of rain and even hail on a Saturday morning which caused extensive flooding. At Sankey Bridges, Liverpool Road became a lake three feet deep, and Wash Lane in Latchford was also, appropriately enough, awash!

1976 was the longest and hottest summer on record, with sunshine every day from June to September, and only $^1/_5$ of an inch of rain falling in August. Warringtonians paid for this twice. Once in September when six inches of rain fell, and again when their water rates went up by 18%.

Perhaps the most stylish piece of modern architecture in the Borough!.
A.E. Howell

Postscript

This book has achieved its aim if it has given pleasure, plus an insight into the diverse development of Warrington from its earliest beginnings to the present time. For, although some of us grumble about the 'warts' and 'carbuncles', it is still our town, and there is much of which we can be proud.